Your 2nd Half After Sports

Your 2nd Half
The Answer
After Sports

*The No-Holds-Barred, Straight-Shooting,
Must-Have Manual for Your Post-Sports Life*

Grayson Marshall, Jr.

All rights reserved. No part of this book may be reproduced, stored, or transmitted by any means, whether auditory, graphic, mechanical, or electronic without written permission of both publisher and author, except in the case of brief excerpts used in critical articles and reviews. Unauthorized reproduction of any part of this work is illegal and is punishable by law.

ISBN-

ISBN-

Library of Congress Control Number: (if needed for libraries)

_____ Publishing date:

(Publisher Logo)

Cover Design by Dr. Adrian A. Gentry

Dedication

This book is dedicated to my sister Dr. Terri Marshall and her unconditional love for me and support in every endeavor I have taken on.

To my children and grandchildren who are my passion for Legacy creation. To the Brothers of A.D.A.A.M. who have held up my arms like Aaron did for Moses.

To every athlete, former and future, I pray this book shifts you, challenges you, and changes you.

Table of Contents

Dedication v
Foreword ix
Do any of these apply to you?.. xiii
Pre-game Show... xv

1st QUARTER: 2nd Half Skill #1 ....**1**

    1: My Game Film 3
    2: Your Game Film 9
    3: Turnovers 21

2nd QUARTER: 2nd Half Skill #2 ....**25**

    4: What It Means to Live in the Present Moment...........27
    5: How to Handle Full Court Press (Life's Blitzes)........37
    6: What is Metacognition and Why Is It Important?.....43

HALF-TIME: 2nd Half Skill #3......................................**49**

    7: Mad Love for the Game 51
    8: Making Game Adjustments 57

3RD QUARTER: 2nd Half Skill #4 ....**61**

    9: No Glitz or Glory, Just Gain 63
    10: Find the Good!..75

4TH QUARTER: 2nd Half Skill #5 79

    11: Be the Brand 81

    12: The After Party – What Does YOUR Brand Look Like? 93

FINAL BUZZER 99

    13: The 5 Indispensable Keys for Your 2nd Half 101

O.T. : (OUTTAKES) 107

    14: Need a Coach? 109

    15: Setting Goals the Right Way 111

    16: Building New Networks 115

    17: Word Traps (Proverbs 18:21) 117

    18: Confidence and Faith are Two Different Things 123

    19: Greed, Ego, and Insecurity 125

    20: Stop Believing Your Press, Instead, Believe Your DNA 127

    21: If you *are* god, why do you need a God? 129

    22: He Didn't Give You Seasonal Ability, But Rather Lifetime Ability 131

    Conclusion: Knowing What I Know Now, What Do I Do Next? 133

    About the Author 135

    Acknowledgments 137

    How to Order 139

Foreword

I first met Grayson in 2019 when he asked me to be a guest on his podcast. It didn't take long for me to recognize his strength of character as we got to know one another before the podcast and also during the time he interviewed me. I witnessed a true professional, sincere in wanting to do the right thing for athletes, and really, for humanity. His passion and willingness to go above and beyond helping athletes thrive in their 2nd Half was evident in everything he said—I walked away, inspired. When he asked me to write the Foreword for this book, I was even more inspired, and humbled.

Grayson is leaving a legacy, and I know a little something about legacies.

I've been able to utilize the legacy my father left me to continue helping people, and with God's help, I daily put the lessons and principles I learned from my parents into practice. Whether I'm on the baseball field for an interview, as a global ambassador for Food for the Hungry, or through my insurance agency, I use the tools I already have in my toolbelt to excel and take my life game to the next level. But I haven't always had the best tools.

When I was a kid in school I couldn't do my homework and most of my tests had to be done orally because there was a disconnect in writing out the answers. I knew the information but I could not assimilate it onto paper. Another major factor was my inability to focus, which continued into adulthood.

About eight years ago I was studying for an insurance test for my agency and I was having issues with focusing. I had experienced fifteen concussions before I entered high school and now as an adult I knew something wasn't right, something was off. I went to The Brain Center in Dallas, Texas to get tested and that was when I was diagnosed with ADD, ADHD, and PTSD. At the time I had no peripheral vision and I had begun experiencing memory loss. At The Brain Center they told me I had been walking around with just 64% of my balance. After only four days of treatment, I had over 84% of my balance and my peripheral vision opened up for the first time since I was a kid.

I've always been adamantly against taking any kind of medication unless absolutely necessary, but I started on medication about three weeks ago as of this writing and I can honestly say it has helped me tremendously. The new tools in my toolbelt for coping with the situation is to follow in my dad's footsteps and help people rise up beyond their circumstances, and that's been a huge blessing in my life. I have found that focusing is much easier when it involves helping others and not focusing on myself.

Your 2nd Half, teaches transitioning athletes to use the tools they already have in their toolbelt to move forward and take ownership of themselves and their lives. In this book, Grayson lays out a clear, power-packed gameplan for how athletes can effectively transition by using the skills they already have… the skills they acquired during their sports career…to live successfully in their 2nd Half.

The core of Grayson's message is to equip athletes to ditch excuses and get their mindset unstuck from the thinking that being an athlete is the *only* thing they know how to do. Grayson charges up athletes with statements like "You just need to do what you did in the first half in a little different way." He doesn't re-invent the wheel. He simply says to take the wheel you already have and roll it in a slightly different direction. That's it.

My dad was my example of excellence and giving to humanity in meaningful, positive ways—he died on his way to deliver supplies to earthquake victims in Nicaragua. His baseball skills were legendary and his giving skills left an impact that I pray will be a generational blessing for our family.

Likewise, Grayson's skills on the basketball court at Clemson were legendary. He has taken those leadership skills and is now impacting multitudes of athletes who are entering their 2nd Half, wondering if they have what it takes to live in "the real world" as well as they did in the sports world. Grayson has lived the dream, he has broken assist records, and he has suffered the barrenness of being a transitioning athlete. In this book, he does not come at the athlete from a high and mighty stance. Instead, he approaches transition from a humble, been-there-done-that mentality while also administering a heavy dose of reality to those who don't quite get it yet. He teaches through the five 2nd Half skills and the five indispensable keys that there is indeed an answer after sports and that you, the athlete, *are* the answer because you already have everything you need to live successfully in Your 2nd Half.

Roberto Clemente Jr.
Former Baseball Player
Former Broadcaster for NY Yankees
Global Ambassador for Food For The Hungry
National Hispanic Health Foundation
Owner of Roberto Clemente Jr. Insurance Agency

Do any of these apply to you?

I can't get out of my current situation but I believe there is a better life for me.

I want to be as successful in my post-sports career as I was during my career but I feel like I don't have the right tools.

I am stuck in the past. I loved my life back then. I loved the people, and everything was so good. Now, I find myself nearly in tears thinking about the past while my present life passes me by.

I know there is a better me deep inside, but I don't know how to develop into a better version of me and I feel stuck.

I feel like I need permission, positive praise and encouragement or *something* every time I try to move forward. I want to be powerful and decisive, and not so dependent on what others think or say about me.

People expect a version of me that I don't really want to be.

People say the quickest way to get from point A to point B is a straight line, but I am stuck at point A and don't know how to move ahead.

I feel like I have to please everyone. I even call myself a people-pleaser but I am not pleased with myself. I want to do things to grow my own life rather than cater to others demands.

I don't think I ever left my family and grew up. I don't think I really know myself well enough to be courageous.

Pre-game Show

This book will give you an eye opening awareness that the game is not over. The game of life is the biggest one we all play in and it is never too late to make new plays, adjustments and develop a winning team. I'm here to tell you that the effort, tenacity, and determination that got you to the game are the same things that will get you the victory in your second half. You just have to know that you're not that far off from your post-sports career success. Since the sports playing field, the court, is so uniquely different, you may think your performance in the latter half of your life will require you to completely unlearn what you already know and learn a ton of new skills. Truth be told, most athletes don't want to unlearn and relearn *anything* because they know what it took to get to the apex of their given sports—they know the hours of commitment, the dedication it took and they don't want to traverse that road again. They know the slippery slope of social media and have experienced the highs and lows. They have experienced it all and they don't want to go through the same things and definitely not start from the beginning. I want you to know that you have more in your arsenal, more in your DNA, that screams success because of what you did as an athlete. You already have the upper hand. The fear and trepidation of starting your life in the second half stems from the fact that you are now navigating through unfamiliar territory. There's no faith or trust in this path because you've never gone this way before.

As a former athlete, you can trust me. As a point guard and a record-breaking assist guy, you can trust me. As an ACC Legend, you can trust me. I've been able to take the non-compromising principles of God and combine them with natural applications of how the world exists and put them together in a book that will help you be encouraged and inspired if you're willing to keep reading.

This book is the bible of applicable instruction for athletes who are intentional about living a winning, successful, purposeful life after sports. The information I put forth in these pages is designed to help you, the athlete, navigate the challenges you will experience during your transition out of sports.

As a former athlete, I really believed I have been created for success. I had no reason not to believe it—I literally had every resource necessary to insure my success. But what I found in the end is that all those resources were not enough to get me where I desired.

This book is not meant to dismiss or negate programs that currently exist, but rather point out how a lack of the *right* resources and tools can prevent you as an athlete from becoming successful after sports. I mean, you *do* expect success to be a part of your post-sports career, right?

Of course, you do! That's why I created this *No-Holds-Barred, Straight-Shooting, Must-Have Manual for Your Post-Sports Life.*

I'm going to give you the *right* tools so you can transition out of sports and into the "real" world with a sense of purpose and accomplishment. You wouldn't dream of using a child's play tool set to build a sturdy, well-constructed house on a solid foundation. You need grown-up tools and the training to use them.

I reiterate that you have the right tools, you must know how to effectively use them to achieve your end goal. What good would a jigsaw or speed square or chalk box be if you didn't know how to use them properly? After all, you needed to effectively use the tools of practice, strategy, teamwork, and the will to win to excel in the sports world. I'm going to show you how those same tools can open the door to an abundance of opportunities and help build good habits you can use the rest of your life—a strong foundation on which to build your post-sports career.

When you enter the sports world, either as a player or coach, it is to shape your own life and also those around you whether teammates or staff. When I look back at my youth and athletic life, I realize there were many areas where I had inadequate information and training. As an older and wiser adult, it is important that I help other athletes gain a clearer picture of where they are presently and a broader vision of who they can become as they transition out of sports. Most athletes after they have played sports at any level are faced with a major decision, "What will I do next?" As an athlete, you know all too well that sports takes full-on commitment, intense passion, and a sold-out mindset; the sports life totally engulfs and dominates your life. When something plays that big of a role in your life for so long, it has become a passion, it's exceedingly difficult to shift gears and to change your mindset. If you have experienced any level of success in the world of sports, downshifting to a "normal" life is even more difficult. You may have become accustomed to a glamorous, financially-rewarding and ego boosting lifestyle sometimes being noted in the upper echelon of celebrities across the country and globe. Statistically, not every athlete reaches that level, and, in fact, a ridiculously small percentage of people actually "arrive."

I want to show you how to deal with life when the glam fades, nobody recognizes you in a grocery store or airport, and your name is on a list with many others whose title is now "former player." When the party's over. When the last whistle has blown. Who will you become?

I confess, I initially handled the transition out of basketball poorly. I didn't have the necessary tools to maintain the success I garnered on the court to become my best off-court self. After spending time working on myself I wanted my 2nd half to be about helping and directing others towards a different, better life; the kind of life that starts with a significant mindset change. I have become known as *The Metacognition Expert*. I decided to use my natural gifting, experience and knowledge-base to help as many people as possible shift their thoughts to one of growth, possibilities and prosperity. So, when I sat down to draft this book, my goal was to provide a framework, a blueprint, in particular, that athletes could apply during their transition from sports into their post-sports life.

THE ANSWER AFTER SPORTS

Put on your toolbelt because I'm going to give you the *right* tools you need and help understand how to use them to perpetually maintain success outside of sports, because there's no way an athlete who committed himself to a certain success level in sports should ever have to live an unsuccessful second half. There's *no way* that should happen.

What I found in my research was that athletes literally live in two separate worlds; they live in the world as an athlete and they live in the world as a non-athlete. To that person, it appears they need two separate game plans, two separate skillsets that are sometimes diametrically opposed. Believe me, I used to think the same thing. I thought the skills I would need outside of sports would be completely different from the ones I used to play basketball. When I decided to go in a different direction, I believed I had to completely reframe and shift my whole mode of thinking and way of operating.

I *thought* I had to think differently about *everything*.

What this book is about is the total antithesis of that train of thought. As a matter of fact, what I'm going to share with you is simple; everything you did to become a world-class athlete is the same things you need to do to create perpetual success in the world outside of sports.

When I was walking and dictating this book, I was thinking about the five keys I shared in my other book, <u>Do. Positive. Just Because. The Keys to the Life You Always Imagined</u>, and how those same five keys/skills apply to the sports world. For the purpose of this particular book I will call them Second Half Skills because you will use each skill to construct a luxury think-box with a sturdy, success-reinforced foundation that will hold your house up during storms and keep you grounded in victories.

I will use sports language and analogies, to highlight the five 2nd Half Skills. As we continue you'll learn that you can use that same language for success outside the sports world; you'll simply learn how to apply some of the words differently. What you may not realize is that you have had these skills the entire time you played sports, so you don't have to completely change your mode of thinking…you just have to shift a bit here and there. That epiphany blew my socks off because I thought I needed different information to live a successful life after I transitioned out of sports. I thought I had to make all kinds of changes. And while it's true you still have to grow in your intellect, you don't have to adapt a whole new way of thinking. Man, if I would have known this stuff when I was leaving basketball, my transition would have been a lot smoother, or at least a whole lot less stressful. I thought I had to reinvent myself, become this totally new person. Why? I based everything on my basketball persona, and I assumed I had to hang the old cape up and become another person. I thought I had to shift from Superman back to Clark Kent and now Mr. Kent was the only person I could be. In reality, what I've come to find out is that I never had to bounce between Superman and Clark Kent, and that I could still be the superhero without the cape. When I finally woke up and began to understand this; man it was revelatory!

When you fully embrace the five 2nd Half Skills listed below you can avoid being among the players who don't leave the league with grace and dignity. Throughout these pages I will expound on each of the five skills and how they can unlock the doors to your better second half. For now, here is an overview:

2nd Half Skill #1 - Study the Film. It is paramount that you study the film of your life because the eye in the sky doesn't lie. You have to own where you are today; no excuses. Studying the film will help you to fully embrace your personal accountability and own where you are now.

2nd Half Skill #2 - Feel the Full Amnesia Effect. You've got to learn to live in the present moment because time is not as important as you think it is.

2nd Half Skill #3 - Have Mad Love for the Game. Or it'll be too easy to hang it up.

2nd Half Skill #4 - Master the FUNdamentals.

2nd Half Skill #5 - Build a Lasting Brand. You have to pay it forward and empower the next generation because you won't be remembered for what you did in the first half, but rather what you did in your second half and who you positively impacted. It is now time to successfully execute your post-sports life.

For those who don't leave their sport gracefully, the underbelly of post-sports life is often splashed on the television screen as we see and hear stories of athletes who have gone broke, who's in jail or who's causing all sorts of drama. These players seem to lack the ability to shift into anything outside sports. I think that's why so many athletes stay inside the sports world in any capacity because it's a comfortable, familiar place.

The one thing about your life after sports is that in order for you to succeed outside that realm, you have to *believe* without a shadow of a doubt that you *can* succeed. You didn't play the first half believing you were going to lose, no, you believed with everything in you that your team was going to win. Now that sports is no longer the focal point in your life, you may be fearful of investing that same amount of time moving into the next chapter of your life. It might have taken you ten, twelve, fourteen years to master your craft and you don't want to put in that kind of time investment to learn something new.

If you've been paying attention to what I have said, you don't have to! You don't have to reinvest the same amount of time. Why? Because you're already doing what it takes, you just have to re-engage your skills in a different way. Application is the key!

<u>Attention:</u> Youth athletes! I strongly recommend you to read this book so you can learn that your journey through sports and out of sports can and does have an exciting and positive flow. Whenever you decide to stop playing, you can move positively and confidently into the next level of your life without having to figure it all out. I'm going to show you the path and give you a beacon of light to illuminate your way! That's why metacognition is so important; it helps you think the *right* thoughts that, in turn, will help you take the *right* actions, that, in turn, will lead you to the *right* success for YOU as an individual.

Metacognition is about teaching people *how* to think, not *what* to think. I will give you the how, so you can apply the principles to all areas of your life. Isn't that exciting? Isn't it going to be fun to know that you can live a life you are truly in control of? You chose the sport you played because of what you love doing. Why would you not live the rest of your life doing what you love to do, without fear, without reservation, without anything holding you back? When you started playing sports, you played with all the passion, all the desire, all that was in you. Your whole life should be that way! I strive to make this book completely different from anything you've read so far, because in addition to motivating you I want to equip you to conquer and rule your own universe—yes, pretty much like a superhero! You might even need to shake out your cape by the time you finish this book.

What you do now, from this moment on, is take the information I'm going to give you and apply it to the life you're living today and every day going forward. I guarantee you when you do that, you will see significant changes. Now, don't get it twisted, just like in sports, you have to do the work. Personal and business success won't just magically appear without you lifting a finger. Your ultimate success lies in you making the changes you need to make as you move from dependency on a system to thinking for yourself.

Athletes, get ready! Your 2nd Half - The Answer *After* Sports blueprint is here!

1st QUARTER

2ND HALF SKILL #1

STUDY THE FILM

1

My Game Film

Since I'm going to cover important aspects of *your* game film in this 1st Quarter, I would be remiss if I did not first share with you the game film on my first half so you know where I'm coming from and just how much I can help you in your second half.

My first half journey may be similar to yours, or it may be completely different from yours, but what I do know is that my first half started me on way toward my purpose and destiny. As a young kid, I strived to excel in sports it didn't matter what sport, I excelled. In academia I also excelled. I was fortunate to grow up in a two-parent home and one of our family focuses was education; black history, world history, and understanding life through the eyes of my parents in middle class America. My Mom was a principal and my Dad was a full-time teacher and he parttime cabbie. My first half was one of sacrifice and hardwork, we did not having everything others had, but we had enough to make me appreciative. My first half involved summer camps, coaching young people and community service. It was during these experiences that I developed good people skills and began to hone my communication and public speaking skills. My first half was also about hard work. It was about expectations. It was about preparation. My first half was about learning to do things the right way. I surrounded myself with other guys who had the same desires, and we all were committed to successfully living our lives.

One of the things my buddies' and I did was commit to being accountability to one another. Our first half was about being the ultimate student-athlete. The first half was about learning everything we needed to learn, both the good and the bad, and especially how to handle adversity. All of these lessons which seemed to be the foundational pieces we would need to have a successful life. Our first half engaged us with challenges and trials. It was a time of expanding ourselves—doing everything humanly possible to position ourselves for a life of greatness.

I grew up attending Catholic school and then an all-boys military school. Why? My parents and I believed the structure of Catholic school and the rigid discipline of military school was paramount for me to prepare for the rest of my life. Military school provided me an upper level education. My sister also had a private school education. This helped me better understand the sacrifices my parents made to position us for a better life.

My high school athletic success led me to college basketball and a scholarship to Clemson University. The Clemson experience broaden my preparation for my post-sports life.

Some people thought I was going to a school that was above my skill level. So I leveled up and learned how to tune out the voices of other people and pursue my dreams based on what was in *my* heart. Tuning out others' voices is a necessary skill to learn in the first half if you want a successful life. Attending Clemson I was a starting freshman, I had earned "ACC Rookie of the Week" four times, won MVP honors at various tournaments, and was the "Holly Farms Player of the Week" on multiple occasions; it was an incredible time. Not only did I excel on the court, I had great two summer internships in the nation's capital for Senator Strom Thurman. The experience in Washington, DC gave me exposure to the political process, and the opportunity to interact and network with politicians and other movers and shakers and have some amazing doors open. I finished my Clemson career as the all-time ACC career assist leader, the all-time Clemson career assist leader, leaving an indelible mark in the Clemson halls of sports and I graduated on time with my degree.

Man the first half was exciting!

There was so much travel domestically and across the globe and I truly believed it was the foundation and preparation I needed for a fulfilling and rich life. After I graduated I returned home to Jacksonville, Florida in 1989. At the time, I wasn't certain why I moved back except I knew my destiny wasn't in D.C. Truthfully, I didn't have a clear plan for my future and found myself still dealing with my first half carryover. Why? Because I figured out that the information and experience I had gained—everything that had been taught to me—didn't sufficiently prepare me for the post-sports life I wanted. See, the harsh reality was that the post-sports life I started was not equipped with the necessary tools to build the second half that I WANTED. I'd been given the blueprint for the latter half *someone else* wanted me to have. Here's what I mean: The pattern and experiences I had were never designed to help me get what I *really* wanted out of life; they unfortunately prepared me for a platform of mediocrity. I didn't realize at the time that I was being programmed, wired, so to speak, for a life that would result in maintaining the status quo. You see, I thought what I had been taught was enough for the great life I envisioned and I did nothing more than enjoy the experience believing I was in the right place. I *thought* I was doing the right things to create my best life. As time went on and I began to be diligent in my quest for personal success, I came to understand that the "system" was set up to create an employee. The "system" wanted me to be part of the masses and to be content with being average—a condition that never felt right to me. I realized that my degree would only reposition me to start over at the bottom again. It was a rude awakening! I prepared for a carryover of my first half success and fell face first into frustration, indecision, and a pile of questions.

What's next?

How do I move forward differently?

Is this really what I signed up for?

Misinformation and miscommunication got me to a place of frustration because when I tried to apply the same work ethic that had allowed me to excel in sports, it did no more than reinforce the average mindset in the world. I thought I was above average. In the world around me, I learned that even if I worked harder than anyone else I still got paid the same amount of money. In sports I was accustomed to standard that the harder you work, the more accolades and recognition you received. So I wasn't prepared for a life of mediocrity!

As an athlete, I strived to never be average. In the sports world you want to stand out, be a superstar - not be average or maintain the status quo. Now if you are alright being an average Joe a part of the status quo, OK. But that wasn't and still isn't for me. Over the past years, I learned through my travels and discussions that people from various walks of life that being average isn't where its at. Many of them weren't athletes but found themselves following the same blueprint for a life of mediocrity and they felt hoodwinked and bamboozled. As I talked to them, I found out that many of them, too, aspired for greatness. They wanted an amazing life! Who doesn't? You hear people say "Well I don't want all that stuff." Baloney! Most people say they don't want a great house, luxury vehicle, incredible vacations, etc. because they believe they can never have them or it will take too much hardwork to achieve. Now I'm not talking about nice things just to have them. When I talk about having the life you've always imagined, I'm talking about having a life with less stress. A life of good physical and mental health. One of loving relationships with family and friends. I'm talking about a life of abundance in every area. I'm talking about a life of giving.

Wow, what a quandary I and so many others found themselves in! We don't want the second half to be like the first, yet unfortunately it is for most people. Because the game plan didn't change at half time, it only continued so we went into acceptance mode. Acceptance that "this is just how it's going to be" and "I'm going to learn to make the best of it". You can't fault your coaches, your parents, or your educators as they were only teaching you what they were assigned to teach you, the same things that were taught to them. It wasn't until I believed there was more to life than where I was and that I sought out different information, tested it and applied what worked that I began to create the second half I wanted. I believe every athlete wants a successful and happy post-sports life. I believe that everyone wants the ability to make positive changes and create a positive outcome. This is what happened for me. And this is what I believe is happening for you, too! You want a successful, happy post-sports life and you want the tools to make positive changes to build your positive outcomes. Now, let's get into the nitty gritty of *your* game film.

2

Your Game Film

As athletes, you know when it is time to go into the film session, everything will be revealed. No matter what you *think* you did in the game, no matter what you *think* happened, the eye in the sky doesn't lie.

There's accountability in the film room. When sitting in the film room with coaches watching and critiquing the entire game, there is no denying errors…it's all right there on the screen. It's that accountability that helps players on the court or on the field. When you're playing sports you are responsible for being on time to team meetings and workouts and for memorizing and executing plays and; all the things necessary for you to continue at the pro level. If you are like me, you had no problem with that—after all, you knew what you had to do to get to that pro level and what kept you there. You were held accountable by a coach, a trainer, or somebody who was employed by the organization to make sure you did the things you needed to do.

If you want to experience a successful transition out of sports there's better way to begin than to study the film of your life. You have to be willing to go in and look at the film for what it is; the good, the bad, and ugly. The objective of this review is to get you to own where you are today; No excuses. No explanations. It is what it is. Nowadays the world we live in and are accustomed to, allows us to make excuses. By making excuses we never get to a place of being fully and personally accountable for our choices and outcomes, which is ironic since as athletes we had to be totally responsible for every aspect we played in the game.

In team sports, there are a lot of players who will say, "It's the other guys fault" when an error or misplay happens. If you want to navigate a better post-sports life, to live a better second half, you must learn to accept full responsible for everything; no matter how a circumstance arrived or how you got to a certain point. What we tend to do is look outside of ourselves for something or someone to blame. Why do we do this? Because we don't want to accept our role in the error or bad situation. Now, granted, a lot of the information we were given wasn't the right information but we actively engaged in a situation or event because we thought it was the right thing to do or we were too lazy to look for a different path. It's in the past. We're talking about the present and how to successfully navigating *our second half.*

Successful navigation of your post-sports life can only begin with first owning exactly where we are today. No excuses... no explanations. Watching our life's game film is a tough thing to do, especially for athletes with big egos, and that's why it's the first skill because if we can't get past this skill we won't make it to the rest of the skills. I have learned from personal experience, if you don't put everything into mastering the first skill, the rest of the skills will remain undeveloped.

You gotta own it! So what does that mean? Does your history have an impact? Yes. Your history can have a long-term impact on how you relate to yourself and others. So you grew up in a low income neighborhood. You didn't have a father or mother to love and support you along the way. You had children out of wedlock. You are divorced. You are working a deadend job. You were given some bad information. So what? Accept it and believe you can have a fresh start, learn some new things and score big in the second half of your life. Continuing to study your game film isn't easy it is difficult to look at our mistakes but it's necessary in order to build a more successful life. Nothing about this book is meant to be soft, fluffy or easy because successful people and successful living requires difficult words, reality checks and doing the necessary work. If it were easy everybody would be doing it so I'm here to get in your face and tell you <u>no</u>, it's not easy but <u>yes</u> it's worth it. You have to engage in some serious self-reflective mirror time in order to get to the next level. Watching game film with other players and coaches, you thought you were in the right position on the field or court and had made the right read. In the moment, that's what it felt like. But under further review, you realize that you missed the mark and totally blew the assignment. Even though you prepared and executed the play to the best of your ability somehow you missed something.

The great ones—Peyton Manning, Tom Brady, Tony Gwynn, Michael Jordan, and Mike Tyson—the top of their sport constantly studied their films. They study the competition. But, more importantly, they studied themselves. They looked at and continually asked themselves *"how I can get better?" "Are my body mechanics right?" "How could I have executed that play more efficiently?"* Why? Because they knew the end result ultimately fell back on them. When you begin to blame others on your team or in society, blame your upbringing, blame other ethnicities, and blame outside influences, you only set yourself up to weaken and diminish your gifts, talents and strengths.

I use many sports examples but my foundation and belief is in the Holy Bible. It's in the things of God. So when you look at what God instilled in you, especially athletes, that's God-given. You have to take personal inventory of where you are. When you've been set on a pedestal, when you've been entitled, when you've been given so much because of your physical ability, when nothing comes to pass or your expectations aren't fulfilled, it's a hard challenge.

The world we live in today, we see more and more people not owning up to anything they do. They have never taken responsibility for their actions. We see this happening with mass-shooters kill dozens of people and then turn the gun on themselves so there is no personal long-term consequences to the shooter's actions. In this entitlement-based society we have practically removed personal responsibility from the equation. The world of social media can make the average person an instant star and the result of a situation going viral can lead to the demise of that individual both personally and morally. Why? Because now they no longer own who they are—they're now defined by how the world sees them. They think it's certainly not their fault for posting something they knew had the potential to explode online. It's the condition of our present society and a world problem.

If you want to be successful in the second part of your life you have to own every aspect of your life. No excuses. No explanations. William Dyer said it best, "Don't complain and don't explain." This is a big statement because a lot of athletes have been spoon-fed since the day someone discovered they had talent. They've been walked down an easier path outside of their own physical responsibilities and have been misinformed and have swallowed the bitter pill of misunderstanding of what's needed in your post-sports life.

I can't even tell you how many athletes have come to me after they have finished their sports career with this declaration "I don't need anything anymore because I'm done playing…I'm finished…I'm over. They don't care about me anymore." I give them their first reality check. I ask, "When are you going to care about *you*?" I try to show them how they're making excuses, and it happens day after day, week after week, month after month. The blame game continues on…we blame the professional organization, we blame the university, we blame all these entities. At the end of the day, if we want to have the life we desire, we have to personally own our current status and take the necessary steps on our journey to make it happen.

You want to be successful? You must be accountable. Own where you are. There are no excuses in the film room! I tell athletes all the time, "If you made an excuse on the field or on the court when a coach questioned you about what happened, how long would you play?" The answer is: You would never get to play.

So why are you making excuses now when you didn't before? When did you get into that habit? It didn't serve you before so why do you think it will serve you now? When you don't make excuses, it's almost impossible for you not to succeed during your second half. You don't think the same principles apply in a different arena and that's why you struggle and fail. The same approach you used on the field, is exactly what you should be doing now. When you started playing football you didn't know everything on day one so why do you think going into your second half that you will know everything from day one? When you start a new job you don't know everything you need to know on the first day even though you may be knowledgeable in the field. It's a new job, a new environment, new rules. It takes time to learn. When you start your post-sports life, yes, you're starting over, but you're starting with a better foundation, with applied skills if you understand how you can use them. I'm trying to tell you you're already doing them! You're already accountable, you did things for your team without even thinking about it so get back to the basics.

Look at the film. Study the film. See where you're at.

The same effort you applied for personal and sports world improvement has to be the first thing you do your life after sports. If you became a professional athlete and mishandled your money, you have to own it. Don't blame your agent. Don't blame the rookie symposium. Don't blame the financial planner you hired. It's on you! You should have learned what it took to help manage your finances. You should have done a better job at being fiscally accountable. <u>YOU</u> should have done that, no one else.

If you didn't get the chance to play sports at the level you wanted, don't blame an injury. If you didn't finish college, don't blame the university. What you have to do is say "Here's where I am today. I've gotta learn to own *all* parts of my life. Right here, right now, my present circumstances is exactly where things are." It's not about whether where you are is good or bad, it just is. I love Romans 8:28. It's an applicable verse to help understand how all the parts of your life fit together. The verse says "And we know that all things work together for good to those who love God, to those who are the called according to His purpose." All things means… drum roll…ALL THINGS! Not some things, not only the good things…ALL THINGS. You might not know how "all" those things are working out for your good, but have faith, knowing that all the circumstances of your life are working for your good if you love God should make your heart race with excitement.

We already know the old formula for success that worked for us as athletes. Because of your physical prowess, because of your athletic skill set, the old formula for success worked.

The formula that was made popular by Napoleon Hill's book *Think and Grow Rich*, which said "focus on what you want, develop a plan and strategy to go get it, and then execute that plan". The old formula, a prescription with a 97% failure rate, was comfortable and familiar. Because of the familiarity there was more faith and when you operate anything by faith it's going to manifest and come to fruition. When it comes to faith, think about it: when you were playing you had faith in the coach and coaching staff, athletic trainers, and the team doctor.

As you know, coaches go from team to team in the NFL; they change every two or three seasons, so in four, five, or six seasons you may have to go through four, five, or six coaches but you're going to have to trust every new coach, that they know what's best for the team. Here's the reality: if you really trust in your skill set, then it doesn't matter who the coach is.

When you exit sports you don't *think* you have the needed skill set to be successful off the field or court. What I want to do with this book is tell you YES YOU DO, have what it takes to be successful off the field or court! There are no two ways about it. YOU DO! You have the same foundation and skills; you just have to seek out a coach to give you the tools to fine tune your existing skill set. You must learn to trust and believe in yourself outside of sports because if you don't trust yourself you will make excuses and operate in fear. And because in our sports life we operated by faith and because we used our willpower, God-given ability, talent, perseverance, and stick-to-it-iveness, we elevated to the upper echelon and became successful. So what happens after sports is we *think* we can apply the same mindset as we did during the active years of our sports career. And let me be clear: mindset and skill set are two different things. Our mindset is how we think. Our skill set is our range of skills and abilities. What we see is that our latter half isn't played out in a sports arena before hundreds of thousands of fans. Nor do we have the same platform and popularity level, and some of use have lost faith in ourselves.

When I am constantly making excuses and not owning up to where I am currently, I lack the necessary faith to move into my new season. When I turned the ball over on the court, which I rarely did, I had to go get it back. I had to have faith that I could go make the next play. Now here's the deal: I could've hit that person right in the hands; I gave them a beautifully bounced pass and they missed it. At that point I have to say, "You know what, I've gotta make a better pass." Even though people look at it and say, "There wasn't anything wrong with that pass, he should have caught it." Here's the deal. If I want to go to a higher level, I have to have enough faith to own whatever happened without excuses.

Let's take football for example. The quarterback has the highest level of responsibility and he has to have the highest level of ownership. When the team wins, he gets credit for the win. When the team loses, he gets credit for the loss. The offensive tackle doesn't. The defensive end doesn't. The wide receiver doesn't. The cornerback doesn't. When a quarterback throws a pass that is dropped, the incompletion goes to the quarterback, not the receiver.

In baseball, the pitcher takes the win or the loss. If there's an error in the field that's not his fault, the person who made the error doesn't take the loss. All pitchers do is win or lose.

Now, in looking at that, the responsibility, the highest level of accountability is on the pitcher. Subsequently, who makes the most money in baseball? The pitchers. Who makes the most money in football? The quarterbacks. The reality of what I'm telling you is that when it comes right down to it, the higher the level of accountability the more you're going to own what goes on, the more success and financial success comes with that.

It works the same outside of the sports arena. People who own a business, who assume the risk, who venture out into entrepreneurism, they're usually the top 1% of wage earners in the world. They often put their own money in the mix yet they still have to hire employees they can direct, they have to comply with local, state, and federal laws on all fronts. But guess who the beneficiary is in the long run? It's the one who's willing to accept by faith the risk that goes with a high level of accountability.

There's no reason for a successful athlete not to be successful after sports. The reason they're not is because they don't understand how to make the shift. Because they are unwilling to do anything different from what got them into sports in the first place. There has to be significant change so again, if you're not willing to change then your life is simply going to be a continuation of using the first half gameplan in your new world that needs a whole new gameplan. Your transition requires a shift from employee and dependency thinking to ownership and individual thought. You must make that shift. Studying the film is critical. If you really want to have a better post-sports career you've got to be intent on studying the film of your life. The great ones live purposely by faith in what they know they can do.

So are you really ready to study the film?

Because once you look at that film, once you really evaluate where you are, then you have no more excuses about what it takes to get to the next level. People who don't want to study the film, who don't want to self-actualize, who don't want to be personally accountable don't go very far.

The bottom line is: Familiarity creates trust. Trust creates faith. I must become familiar with *me and where I am*. I must accept my new starting point so I can move to higher ground. Study your life's game film over and over again. Own where you are today and you have the first skill to successfully living an empowered life—personal accountability.

As we explore exactly what a successful post-sports career looks like, you'll notice it's not all smooth sailing…there are some fumbles and turnovers along the way. These challenges are meant to teach us, to slow us down, and to steady us so we can move forward fully aware, fully receptive, fully willing to accept everything that is about to come into our lives.

3

Turnovers

The shift in the second half doesn't come without some turnovers. When I entered my post-sports career, there was no coach giving me a game plan, no one telling me to work out at specific times or to monitor and make sure I was training in the right way to excel. In May 1988 when I finished playing basketball at Clemson, I still had no idea what I wanted to do so I returned home to D.C. and my "old-school" parents whose mantra was *"my house, my rules"*. By then I had been living on my own too long to go back to that kind of structure. I knew I would fall into, what I would consider the trap, my parents helping me get started in their career path and me getting stuck. I decided I would rather try something new and fall on my face than be stuck so I moved to Florida and began to build my own life. I had a desire to be an entrepreneur so I got into a business that ultimately failed and I found myself homeless at twenty-eight-years-old. I learned the hard way that I needed more, new information and the knowledge on how to apply it. Now, I'm not talking about the kind of homelessness where I was pushing a cart and sleeping under a bridge but I didn't have a place to call my own; I lost everything I had. I was renting a room out of my ex-girlfriend's mom's trailer for ten dollars a week.

If I wanted to get to the success level of the top three percent of the world, I had to get some new information and develop the skills to apply what I was learning. I knew the great ones, whether in sports or in business, these individuals knew a little more than the average person. I knew that average people relegated themselves to mediocrity and really didn't have a desire for any more than they currently had. I also knew that wasn't who I was.

Your second half is going to shift when you come to a new level of awareness that motivates you to engage and apply it to your life.

After being homeless, I discovered that the information I needed to succeed was readily available, and I took it—information that I'm sharing with you throughout this book. I literally began to make the most of every single day. I believe that when you give somebody the *right* information, and they see the truth behind it, and you give them the *right* tools to apply it, they have no recourse but to act. Because the essence of a man, the essence of a woman is to do and be the best that they can be. It doesn't take a lot to shift. It doesn't take a lot to be a little bit better today than you were yesterday. What it does take is gaining some critical information that most of us aren't privy to and don't know how to get, or if we did get it, we wouldn't know how to use it.

THE ANSWER AFTER SPORTS

The prescription for success, or I should say failure, that I previously told you about—develop a plan, strategize to get it, and then execute that plan—well, the first two parts of that plan focus on what you want and develop a plan and strategy to go get it—contain an expectation of an external end result of which until that end result is reached or achieved, it literally puts you in an anxious, stressful existence. So now the first part of the formula is creating more of a problem than it's resolving. The third part of that plan—execute it—is focused on your willpower. We know from research that our willpower is only five percent of our thinking process so the flawed model we are given to succeed is actually creating anxiety and only using five percent of the capability of my mental state to bring it to pass. *That*, my friend, is a formula for failure but since it's the one we've been given most often we swallow it hook, line, and sinker. The model I'm talking about is the one that's been downloaded to so many of us in seminars, in leadership programs and the reality of that model is that it actually does work for about three percent of the people. But what about the ninety-seven percent who want a successful part two of life yet continue to use a flawed model. Turnovers happen with a flawed model. Expectations remain unmet. Hope wanes. Same as me, you find yourself unprepared to overcome life's turnovers which can include relationship troubles, baby mama drama, personal or family tragedy, and business failure. The flawed model gets into your brain and causes havoc but it's the only one you know so you keep plugging away.

When you apply the flawed model and it doesn't work, you're back overwhelmed with frustration. I wanted to be ready for my post-sports career as so many of you do, but there was so much false information, I had to dig through, so much I had to uncover, so much I had to unlearn from the first half that it took me some time to really get to where I needed to be in the second half.

The good news is once you get there, oh my God it's an amazing place!

You'll know if you're successfully living in your post-sports space if you're applying new information, new skills, new techniques, new philosophies, new paradigms. If you're still stuck on average, you're still in the first half. The second half comes after halftime. Halftime is when you make the transition.

Fact one: life has turnovers. Fact two: turnovers don't have to derail your forward momentum or sideline your plans. In the 2nd Quarter I'll give you more tools to help you towards an astronomical post-sports career.

2nd QUARTER

2ND HALF SKILL #2

THE AMNESIA EFFECT:

4

What It Means to Live in the Present Moment

The Amnesia Effect directly relates to living in the present moment because time is not as important as you think it is. When you look at the Amnesia Effect, the great players, the successful athletes in the world always play the games with a case of amnesia, they always do it. They totally forget about the last thing that happened, the last thing they did. They totally forget about the last shot they took. They forget about the last turnover they made. They forget about the last free-throw. They forget about the last missed kick. They forget about the last swing.

In order for you to become successful, you have to learn to live in the present moment consistently. Again, this should not be hard for athletes, but for some reason, outside of the sports world it becomes difficult. It becomes challenging. During the 2016 NCAA tournament between Villanova and North Carolina, and yes as an ACC guy I was rooting for North Carolina, but Villanova had one hell of a team. Chris Jenkins, a homeboy who went to Gonzaga University hit the buzzer beater. They could have felt deflated when Tarheel's Marcus Paige hit a double pump 3 with 4.7 seconds left in the game. But Villanova stayed strong. In the present moment, they executed and Chris Jenkins hits as he says, "A 1-2 step 3-pointer and knocked it down." We've seen this happen time and time again. Last-second shots by an NBA player. Late inning home runs by a MLB player. An NFL field goal is made with less than five seconds on the clock.

All those incidences are a result of the Amnesia Effect which is putting away what's already happened, even a moment ago, and living in the present moment. Thinking, *here's where I have to be*. It's common to be in the present moment in sports. What we need to realize is that when we get outside of the sports arena, we still have to operate with the Amnesia Effect—in the present moment.

Unfortunately, for so many athletes, they don't know how to live in the present moment of their everyday lives because they still want to stay mentally and emotionally attached to a sports they no longer play. They want to be defined by what and who they used to be. They want to live in that old space. Why? Because the old space is comfortable. The old space is familiar. They trust that space, and it is just easier to remain in comfort and familiar places so, they don't move forward. They're not in the present moment—they're living in the past. That's like driving your car and constantly looking in the rear view mirror—you can't effectively go forward without crashing. So what do most athletes do? They never move forward.

THE ANSWER AFTER SPORTS

They stay stuck. They apex in life at the culmination of their sports career. The statistics prove it—in the world of sports we live in today, with the financial rewards athletes are receiving contractually for playing sports, they should be able to move forward successfully in whatever they want to do. But because many of them lived irresponsibly, they more often than not lose almost everything they have. Living in the present moment, with an eye towards the future, is a mature way of approaching the next part of your life. When you lose what you have, it's because you haven't developed a forward thinking financial mindset yet. As I've said, as an athlete you're already living in the present moment. You're just not living in it maturely all the time. What you might have found is that because you lived in the present moment, squandered money, spent it like it was a never-ending source, you want to stay back in that illusional world. Your attitude is what has to shift. Living in the present moment involves moving forward and taking things day by day and redefining and understanding goal setting.

You must set new goals moving into this next part of your life. This is the present moment. All that old behavior needs to be put behind you; all the recklessness is gone. Your new present moment is with a new mindset and a new understanding. Again, having the Amnesia Effect, living in the present moment, is not that difficult because you've lived there during sports. You know what it's like. Same as in the example of North Carolina and Villanova, you can't let what looks like defeat hold you back or hold you down. You can't sit there and think, *well, it looks like failure has beaten me, I think I'll just give up*. Because you're reading this book and you've taken the time to study your film, you've accepted where you currently are in your post-sports world, now you're prepared mentally because you've learned to shift your thinking from instinct to intelligence. Since you're now living in the present moment of your second half it's time to redefine goals.

For most people, when we set goals the way we've been taught to set goals, we give our goal a deadline. Again we're back to the old philosophy of success which worked when it was based on instinct. Remember the Napoleon Hill plan to set a goal, strategize to get it done and then execute it? It doesn't work that way when you approach goal setting with intelligence. The old philosophy, of goal setting, planning steps and locking it down with a deadline, literally creates anxiety, frustration, fear, and negativity.

Going forward, our goals must be defined in a different way. I read an amazing book called *Beyond Willpower* by Alexander Lloyd and he really opened my eyes to a lot of things I share around the world today. In *Beyond Willpower* Lloyd talks about the power of goal setting but the real significance in what he writes is such a strong reflection of athletes; if you begin to make a shift as you're transitioning out of the sports world, you'll have nothing but success in the regular world. See, you were already doing things this new way in the sports world, you just didn't know it. The way Alexander Lloyd talks about defining and setting goals is a 4-step process that I'll talk more about in Chapter 15:

Now, in the sports world we have long-term goals, but watch this. Alexander Lloyd is talking about those long-term goals lining up with what you do consistently on a regular basis. There has to be what I call your *Do Positive Passion* that lines up with Alexander's 4-step litmus test in order for it all to work. It's amazing how sports already sets the foundation for his goal setting method, so again if it seems peculiar that athletes fall so far when their sports careers are over, it's only because they don't really know how close they are to reaching their goals.

There is a short impactful book by Russell Conwell called, *Acres of Diamonds*[1]. The book is based on a parable Conwell heard in 1869 while traveling down the Tigris River, through what is known as present-day Iraq, and in summary it goes like this:

There was once a wealthy man named Ali Hafed who lived not far from the River Indus. "He was contented because he was wealthy, and wealthy because he was contented." One day a priest visited Ali Hafed and told him about diamonds.

Ali Hafed heard all about diamonds, how much they were worth, and went to his bed that night a poor man. He had not lost anything, but he was poor because he was discontented, and discontented because he feared he was poor.

Ali Hafed sold his farm, left his family, and traveled to Palestine and then to Europe searching for diamonds. He did not find them.

---

[1] http://bestbookbits.com/acres-of-diamonds-by-russell-conwell/ (Retrieved 8/14/2019)

His health and his wealth failed him. Dejected, he cast himself into the sea.

One day, the man who had purchased Ali Hafed's farm found a curious sparkling stone in a stream that cut through his land. It was a diamond. Digging produced more diamonds—acres of diamonds, in fact. This, according to the parable, was the discovery of the famed diamonds of Golconda.

He was around during the time where the diamond was the thing to have. So he sold his property and went out on a quest to find the most lucrative place that diamonds existed. He wanted to find it. He sold everything and he went out for years looking for the mother lode of diamonds. Ultimately he never found it. He came back to his home and he walked into his home which was now occupied by somebody else and asked the guy. He looked up on the mantle and saw this huge rock. He walked over to it and looked at it. He found that it was one of the purest diamonds he'd ever seen and it was huge. He asked the guy, he said "Where'd you get this?" He said "Oh there are thousands of them in the creek back there. They're just rocks." The guy didn't even know what he had, but the guy who went looking for diamonds didn't realize how close he was to them because they were right in his own backyard.

Athletes, I'm speaking to you.

The necessary shift for you to become successful after sports is right in your own backyard! You're already doing the process and practices that need to take place for you to become successful. You just need to be shown how to make the shift. How to dig for diamonds in your own backyard. You just need a new game plan and that's what this book gives you—a new game plan! When you add to your life the five skills plus the five indispensable keys we will cover within these pages, I'm telling you, you'll never be the same.

If you study the film, if you maintain the Amnesia Effect, if you learn how to handle the full court press (life's blitzes) which is coming up in the next chapter, you're almost all the way there.

No athlete worries about the last play and becomes successful. You cannot worry about the last thing you did; you literally have to have amnesia. Somebody just scored a touchdown on you—forget about it because you have to come back and make the next play. That's living in the present moment. For some reason when you get out of sports you worry about the next "play," about your next job, the next thing you have to do. Why are you doing that? You've never done that before.

If I've missed ten shots in a row I can't worry about it. Focus on making the eleventh shot is my goal. The amnesia effect is part of you living right now, it's part of you being intentional, it's being in the present moment. I'm taking this action; I'm making that decision for a specific reason.

If you worry about what you just did, you'll never be effective because the only moment you can control is the one you're in right now. When guys come to me saying, "Woe is me, I got baby mama drama, I got alimony, I got too much on my plate," I tell them, "When you're playing football, you got a man in motion this way, you've got a guy doing this, a guy doing that, and you still find the ball don't you? You've got 80,000 people screaming, fireworks shooting off, loud noise; on top of whatever you're carrying personally and you block it all out to run that play. Why? You are aware of all the distractions around you that are there well after the play is over." In your post-sports career, all of life's distractions take hold of you because you don't have your focus where it should be... your next action, your next decision.

Whatever you think about you bring about so focusing on all the drama around you makes each situation appear overwhelming. Whatever has your focus has your momentum so when you're constantly thinking about the negative stuff, and that is exactly what will show up. All these things are part of the mental approach to the Amnesia Effect. It's really understanding that the capacity for thinking a certain way is going to produce results.

It comes down to executable action but to succeed you must talk with somebody who's been doing what you want to do successfully. For example, you decide you're going to start a business. You meet with the right people and applying their sage advice and knowledge, you end up starting a business. Let's say you have a business partner and that partner is less than ethical and you lose the investment. What are you going to do about it? You cannot worry about what happened at that point, rather, ask yourself, *what can I do about it right now*? What steps can I take *right now* to resolve the issue?

I think when things happen to us we want to focus on the bad that happened yet at the end of the day it's not bad if you really consider it a learning experience. It's no different than being hazed as a rookie; it's part of the process. You must understand that's just how it is. We can't hold grudges.

We need to look at our lives and ask, *why am I not living present moment*? If you're thinking about the past and worried about the future, that doesn't mean you don't prepare for the future. Financially, you should be preparing for the future. Healthwise, you should be preparing for the future. You just can't worry about everything because you could be financially prepared, nutritionally prepared and one day be hit by a bus. You can't control every circumstance. If you walk around worried about getting hit by a car, that's what's going to happen. If you're on the field or court and worried about missing shots, or missing tackles, guess what? You're going to miss shots or tackles!

When it comes to the Amnesia Effect time is not as important as you think it is because you're living in the present moment. In order to put that into perspective think of it this way: when you forget about the last thing you did you're now living with a mentality of patience. You're not rushing anything, you're not rushing *into* anything, and that's what the Amnesia Effect creates—the ability to relax because we know it's not over yet; there's more to do. When we rush, we act like time is very important. It's crucial that we slow down because the quicker the transition, the more mistakes you will make. That means you literally have to slow down this moving forward machine and live in the present moment. The Amnesia Effect allows you to do that because it makes you forget about the past and causes you to live in the present moment; not in a rushed state but taking the right action at the right time. It's living with intention. It's living on purpose.

Now it's time to move on and learn how to handle full court presses. Life has a way of bringing those into our sphere, often at a moment's notice. We're blindsided. We're devastated. Now that you have a better grasp of what living in the moment means, you will be better equipped to handle full court presses.

5

How to Handle Full Court Press (Life's Blitzes)

In basketball the full court press is a defensive tactic designed to rush you; make you feel hurried. Its purpose is to catch you off guard. Full court press expects you to not think clearly and make rash decisions based on something that's suddenly thrown at you. Likewise, in football, a blitz is a tactic used by the defense to disrupt pass attempts by the offense. During a blitz, a higher than usual number of defensive players will rush the opposing quarterback, to try to tackle the quarterback or force him to hurry his pass attempt. Often, a quarterback will never know where a blitz is coming from, but good quarterbacks and good basketball players are always prepared for the blitz and full court press. Why? Because they've literally gotten to a place where they're not afraid of anything. They're so prepared that an opposing player or team executing the full court press or the blitz is par for the course. These players live in a world where they're so in tune to prediction, they can, most of the time, forecast the press or blitz before it happens so that literally when it does happen the play doesn't have the result that was intended; to derail them, to knock them off their thought process, to change the way they're thinking for the moment, to make them panic.

The only way for a player or team to handle a full court press or blitz is prepared ahead of time and they know how to respond. They've studied the film. They know who they are. They know what's going on around them. So when the full court press or blitz comes, there's no stress.

For the athlete making a transition, when life's press and blitz's happen to them, it stagnates them, frustrates them…. Why? Because they don't know how to handle it. They haven't prepared. As an athlete we've played the game by instinct. It's what we've done for so long but how does instinct become a part of what we do? Repetition. Studying our life's game film. The more we execute what's familiar, the more faith we have in it. Instinctively, when I made a pass, when I made a steal, when I did something on the court, it had everything to do with repetition. I had done it before. There was never any fear, never any hesitation and never any concern about the outcome that was ultimately manifested. I had a 3.2 to 1 assisted turnover ratio, I didn't turn the ball over because nothing bothered me. Nothing surprised me. I played by instinct.

If you want to live your post-sports life the way you need to, then you have to shift from instinct to intelligence. You have to make a significant mental move from what's familiar to what is new, different, and maybe foreign to you. Instinct is a natural reaction based on what you already know. You see, you react; that's just how it works. In order for you to successfully move into part two of your life instinct won't work in the new world that you've entered into. In this new world you need a new level of intelligence. You need a new awareness of how to shift from instinct to intelligence.

So what are some of life's presses and blitzes? They can include relationship trauma with your significant other or within your circle of family or friends, baby mama drama, personal or family tragedy including accidents, sickness and death, natural disasters, trouble with the law, suddenly getting let go from a job, and business failure which can ultimately lead to financial failure. Life's presses can also include unexpected health issues like cancer, Multiple Sclerosis, Parkinson's, acquiring a sudden physical deformity or limb loss, or other serious health problems. Any press or blitz, even seemingly minor ones like a new reaction or different perception from the public in your post-playing days can feel devastating if you're not prepared.

The presses and blitzes are there to cause you to react. They're there to bring about panic and make you take haste action. If you react too quickly you'll turn the ball over, you'll make mistakes, you'll do the wrong things. But if you understand what you're doing, and have prepared for what life throws at you, you will be more likely to respond accordingly. And notice I said respond, not react. The reason you may *react* and not respond is because fear is more prevalent than faith during those moments. In life's press or blitz instances, you find that your EQ (Emotional Equation) not your IQ (Intelligence Equation) is at play.

Anything that happens in your life, if you believe in the sovereignty of God, although you may not understand the circumstance, you learn to trust it will all work out for your good. You may not like it but you respect it. At the end of the day the whole premise of the Amnesia Effect is not getting caught up in what you can't control. Any situation or event that has a traumatic effect on you is going to be devastating and the truth is that you have no choice but to deal with it, however, if you stay in that negative headspace, it will rob you of your peace, your balance, and your forward momentum.

Since your goal is to be successful, the more hell you have to go through, and as you're going through the presses and blitzes just know that somebody is watching you to see how you handle the situation. They might be watching you so they can gain some hope for their own situation. In the Bible, Job lost everything and his wife and friends were watching him come to total ruin. His wife told him to curse God and die and his friends told him it was all because of his sin. Job's response was, "The Lord gives and the Lord takes away, blessed be the name of the Lord." His response was simply his understanding of the sovereignty of God. If you want to be successful outside of sports, you're going to have to go through some *stuff* outside of sports. That's just how it goes. Are you going to be like everybody else or are you going to learn to handle what comes at you differently? Yes, I know you're only human but as an athlete, whether fair or unfair, you're held to a higher standard, therefore you should handle your full court presses and blitzes with dignity and grace so your testimony can a great one. You're ready for the full court press, you're ready for the blitz, you're ready to eliminate fear. Why? Because you were born that way. The Bible says that God did not give you the spirit of fear, but of power and love and a sound mind.

In the next chapter I'm going to talk about metacognition and what it means and why it's so important. So keep reading because we're getting into some real meaty information that will impact your everyday life forever.

6

What is Metacognition and Why Is It Important?

Metacognition by definition is an understanding and awareness of how you think and it is a needed foundational action to make the shift from instinct to intelligence. My mission statement states, "Elevating lives through the practical transfer and application of knowledge and understanding that translates into life-changing thoughts, perspective and actions."

During your sports career you never had to process anything, you just reacted instinctively to how you were trained. Now, in your post-sports life, you have to understand how your brain's computer actually works outside of the instinctive place in which you've always engaged it. That's what you're going to learn in this chapter—how your conscious and subconscious minds work and how you can get them to work together for your good.

When you look at your brain and the way the mind works, we can go to the Bible for answers. It says in 1 Corinthians 15:46 "However, the spiritual is not first, but the natural, and afterward the spiritual." Clearly we see that we operate first in the natural realm and then in the spiritual." As you begin to understand this truth, you'll see that you were actually doing this as an athlete and now you just need to learn how to turn your brain on in a new area. I've been called The Metacognition Expert because I know a thing or two about how the brain works and how to get it to work the most efficiently for optimum benefit. I like to use a quote that says, "You cannot see the wind directly, you see only its effects. The same applies to your thoughts." There are two components to the way your brain works. There's a subconscious mind and a conscious mind. Your conscious mind is 5% of your thinking. Your subconscious mind accounts for 95% of your thinking. Your subconscious mind is a million times more powerful than your conscious mind. The following is a breakdown of what the conscious and subconscious mind houses in your brain: (I'll talk later on about the 95 horses and this will become clearer)

CONSCIOUS MIND: 5%

1. Analyses
2. Thinks and plans
3. Short-term memory

SUBCONSCIOUS MIND: 95%

1. Long-term memory
2. Emotions and feelings
3. Habits, relationship patterns, addictions

4. Involuntary body functions

5. Creativity

6. Developmental stages

7. Spiritual connection

8. Intuition

The breakdown above explains why athletes excel like they do—because their subconscious mind is inundated by positive thoughts of the sport they love. Their subconscious mind thinks *only* about that sport whether it be basketball, football, golf, tennis, or whatever. So what the Law of Attraction gurus tell us is absolutely true—what you think about you bring about. When you got involved in sports, you only saw the good. You didn't see the negative. You heard stories about the negative aspects of sports, but that's not what you looked at or focused on. You didn't get into sports for the negative, you got into sports for the positive. The reason the sports world is so attractive, the reason that sports in general is so attractive and why parents want their kids involved in sports is because the majority of the time it is a positive experience. Now understand this: When we're talking about the subconscious mind, you have to understand that your brain works on frequency. Each and every person in this world emits a frequency. The thing you must understand is that like frequency will always find like frequency. The world we live in, the technology era, all of us have cell phones. Right now, in Jacksonville Florida, I can call California, I can call my man Norman Noel in the OC. There are no wires to affect the call, it's just frequency finding frequency. If you understand how technology can create a coast to coast connection with no wires, then you understand the power of your brain and how it's thousands of times more powerful than any cell phone. Your brain, when it focuses on the positive, when it focuses on successful outcomes, when it focuses on the good, good is going to happen. You're going to automatically connect with other people who have the same mindset as you, the same frequency as you. **What I'm talking about here is the mindset that you must cultivate and own in your second half.** It's a mindset rooted in faith. So what happens is if you find that your sports career has ended due to retirement or injury or whatever reason, the immediate emotion that's most often triggered is fear. Fear and faith cannot coexist, they're polar opposites.

Fear is an emotion that is only meant to be experienced when you're in a life threatening situation. It is not an emotion you're supposed to deal with on a regular basis. And really, as an athlete you haven't had to deal with fear as your modus operandi, you have dealt far more in faith. You've been operating within sports with the right mental framework but when you get to a place that's unfamiliar, your post-sports career, the new world of intelligence outside of instinct, you feel like you're not equipped to handle things when you've really been handling things the whole time, just under a different mental framework. Going into your part two of life and executing it successfully is simply a matter of making a shift from instinct to intelligence. It's using the power of metacognition to shift your subconscious into hyper-drive. It's the same philosophy and mental approach that you've been used to; it's just that nobody has ever explained it to you this way and nobody has ever introduced it to you in this way. All along you thought you had to do a major mental overhaul into a completely different mental realm. I'm telling you it doesn't take that much to make the shift. In fact, there are three primary things that need to happen:

1. You need to become aware of the shift that needs to be made which is why metacognition is so powerful.
2. You need to know how to make the shift.
3. You need to simply redirect what you've been doing.

You've been living by faith and now you're living in fear because this new experience is all new to you. Understand that fear is the culprit keeping you from executing what you need to do to make the shift to get back to faith. How? Implement what I call the Agape Effect. The Bible says in 1 John 4:18 that "perfect love casts out all fear." Think about it. You were already executing the Agape Effect in a different way in sports because you had a perfect love for the sports world. You weren't afraid of anything; you did your job at whatever position you played. It was an Agape "unconditional love" for the game so you didn't mind putting the work in. You didn't mind going that extra mile because you had nothing but unconditional love for the sport.

Now that you're out of the day in and day out sports element, it's time to shift to perfect unconditional love for yourself. You've got to have that same perfect love for who you are as an individual, a person in the universe—the you who's been thought of and created in God's mind before the foundations of the earth. The new you that's shifting—you've got to love that guy too. You've got to have perfect love for the new place you're going…you've got to unconditionally love yourself not based on circumstances or conditions but simply on who you are as a human being. As an athlete, it didn't matter who you were playing against, it didn't matter what gym you were in, it didn't matter what state you were in; you were going to overcome because of the deep love you had.

If you have a deep love for changing the rest of your life, an unconditional love for living your part two of life, then make that shift back to faith. Nobody has ever brought it to you like this but I get it, I feel you, because I've been there. Maybe this is your story: you started to believe there was nothing else you could do in life except play sports so after that gig was over you fell into mediocrity, into status quo. But deep down you know you were different from the beginning or you wouldn't have reached the level you reached in sports. In the previous chapter I talked about handling the full court press and being ready for what the world is going to throw at you. If you realize that you have already been prepared for "the press" then now, right now, this moment, use what you already possess—unconditional love—and reframe your mental space, and you've got this thing beat.

HALF-TIME

2ND HALF SKILL #3

MAD LOVE FOR THE GAME

7

Mad Love for the Game

When you play a sport, you eat, sleep, and breathe that sport. You play electronically every chance you get. The sport dominates your every thought. You've got mad love for the game—it consumes you 24/7/365. The major key after sports for an athlete is to find *one endeavor* that dominates your thoughts, *that one venture* that captivates your interest, your passion, your motivation.

The question to ask yourself is: what is it I want to do in my post-sports life that will captivate my passion, my thoughts, my motivation? What is *that new thing* I want to do that will fuel me into an unquenchable fire of action? You may ask: do I want to stay within the sports realm, and, if so, what does that look like? Do I want to jump out of sports? Do I want to do something totally different?

It's imperative that you quickly figure out what will give you the same enthusiasm and passion for your new endeavor. What happens with athletes is that they pour so much of themselves into sports that they don't think they have room nor time for another endeavor—they've spent all their physical and mental and emotional resources on that one thing. They think, *I don't have time to develop another life passion.* Think about it. You've undoubtedly been in football or basketball or whatever sport since about six years old and now you're thirty-one-years-old; you've been playing for thirty-five years. You know how long it took to perfect your skill, you know the struggles you've endured along the way, the challenges you've overcome and you ask, "Do I want to learn something new for the next twenty-five years before I truly understand it? In that case the answer is no. More often than not, the response is, "Nah, I don't really want to do that. I'm just going to ride the money out." What got you to the pinnacle of your sport is your passion, your love, your drive. If you want to be successful after sports, you've got to find that *new thing* that you eat, sleep, and breathe; the *thing* that gets you up in the morning. I know I said quickly find it and that is true but that's once you've done your homework and spent time exploring various avenues, businesses, and ventures that interest you. Once you have the information you need, then it's time to decide quickly so you don't get stuck in the analysis paralysis game. If necessary, enlist the help of an outside career counselor or, if you're still playing, set a meeting with your team's Director of Player Engagement. Look online, take career assessment and personality tests to determine your gifts and talents apart from sports. Solicit the help of a metacognition expert.

THE ANSWER AFTER SPORTS

The time to start thinking about your post-sports career is when you enter college, or before. If you're in the pro's, the time to begin planning your exit strategy is the day you get signed to a team. In the world of products, there is "planned obsolescence." It's defined as "a policy of producing consumer goods that rapidly become obsolete and so require replacing." In the world of sports you start becoming obsolete the day you enter college or the pros. Your team is seeking to replace you if you no longer perform up to their standards. That's why I'm trying to help you! It's imperative that you find out at the BEGINNING of your sports career what else you would like to do and begin preparing then. Get around other business people who are in the same business as you. Athletes live in a misnomer world that their sports career is going to go on forever but the truth is every athlete is one injury away from becoming a former athlete or you're simply going to age out so what are you going to do…now?

Having mad love for the game is embracing the sacrifice that's required to become successful in sports and take that same sacrifice and embrace it outside of sports. I ask you again: what are you going to do? Your answer becomes the quintessential challenge. Unfortunately, most athletes rest on their laurels, most of them don't do anything and I really don't get it. When you have mad love for the game you can bring in 1 John 4:18 as I did in the previous chapter, "Perfect love casts out all fear." When you've got perfect love for a new endeavor you can sink your heart and soul into you don't fear anymore. But the brutal truth is that many times athletes don't have perfect love for their new endeavor; it's something they *maybe* feel like doing, something they're going to try casually or maybe even haphazardly, and in the middle of their halfhearted efforts resides fear, not love.

I know one thing for certain: we make bad decisions when we come from a place of fear. During your playing days if you had mad love for the game and you experienced fear, your skillset would overcome it. After sports, the fact that you ran the fastest time ever doesn't matter—nobody cares what you ran or how much you could bench press.

The same mad love has to be a true and passionate embrace of the next thing you're doing because life dictates that you're going to play the game of life more than you'll play the game of football or basketball or whatever sport you play. You know the rules of the sports game you played but you don't know the rules of this new game so you have to learn and that's what I'm giving you in this book—I'm giving you the pieces that work with the new rules. It's like if we sat down and played poker. If you're playing 7-card Draw and I'm playing Texas Holdem, we're both playing poker but you're going to lose because I'm playing Texas Holdem moves. You might say, "Man, I don't know what's going on, I'm playing poker but I'm losing." You're playing with a different set of rules! The rules over here are this. The rules over there are that. Different set of rules. So when you go to a grocery store and no one recognizes you, or there's no fanfare, that mad love for the game will give you a passionate "I don't care" attitude. Instead, you'll think *I've got a new agenda, a new journey, and I don't have time to worry about anyone else."*

THE ANSWER AFTER SPORTS

When you played your sport you didn't care what people said about you; you went out and proved yourself on the field or court. If you wanted to go out and run at four o'clock in the morning in the rain, you did it—you didn't care one iota what anyone thought and it didn't matter if it didn't make sense. You went above and beyond. When you were playing sports, people may have asked, "Why did you play hurt?" You respond, "Mad love for the game!" After sports, people will ask, "Why did you start that business or why did you buy that franchise?" You still respond, "Mad love for the game. I'm not going to lose!"

8

Making Game Adjustments

You just finished playing the first half and your team is losing. Your offense can't seem to move past the other team's defense and your defense can't stop the other team's offense—it's like they have your number and are exploiting it all over the field or court. As you walk into the locker room, the staff tosses you a towel, you grab a cup of Gatorade, and you sit down while the coach agitatedly takes off his sport coat, throws it at his assistant coach and begins to write on the white board what happened in the first half. The ugly truth is all over that board!

You sit there reflecting and listening intently. Why? Because you know there's going to be some new information, there's going to be some adjustments to the game plan. Language laced with colorful superlatives or expletives, the coach points out mistakes made and all the ways the other team is dominating. He then delivers some serious game adjustments so you guys can go back out and play better in the second half.

People, it's the same thing in life.

You're tired. You're frustrated. The first half of your life didn't go as you thought it would go and now you're sitting in life's locker room ready for some new information. Ready to receive what you need to get back out and effectively play part two of your life, now with the necessary plan to win. You've made some adjustments and that's what halftime is…a critical place in your life. Halftime is a critical place in *any* game. Great coaches make adjustments once they realize what they were doing wasn't working. Now, let me be clear, there will always be players and coaches in life that are hard headed. What I mean by that is that they're going to stick to what they said no matter what. Their mentality is *we're going to live or die this way*! As a result of that same mentality there is a whole society of people who are dying—they're dying with their religious beliefs, dying with their life philosophies, dying with their belief systems and no intention of making any adjustments. They're dying with their perceptions firmly set in stone because they're unwilling to change. They're unwilling to do anything different. We've all heard the definition of insanity—doing the same thing over and over and expecting different results. Well, Albert Einstein eloquently put it a different way. He said "You can't fix a problem with the same mind that created it." You can't get different results it you're thinking the same way. If you think the way you're thinking is exactly right, then you are exactly right in your own mind and nothing will ever change. Don't get me wrong, you'll have periods of success but you'll always end up back in the same place. Why? Because you've done nothing different. You've made no adjustments.

If you fall back into the plan from the first half which most people do, your thought process will be something like *whatever changes need to happen, need to happen expeditiously because I'm running out of time*. The majority of athletes live in their first half plan on a daily basis. They don't really approach halftime the right way. In this book you are receiving new information. As an athlete myself, I'm telling you what it's going to take to make your second half a game changer for the better. But it's only going to work if you're open to new information. If you're so stuck on what you believe to be right, and *this is the way I've always done it, this is the way it worked before, this is what everybody teaches, this is what I feel works*, then none of this new information is going to work for you. But if you're willing to hear me out and keep reading, I'm going to continue to show you how to make game adjustments.

There's a new level you must go to in the second half.

There must be more energy in the second half.

There must be more awareness in the second half.

There must be more faith in the second half.

There must be more of a desire to make things happen in the second half.

There must be more patience in the second half.

Taking full advantage of every opportunity must happen in the second half.

Unconventional approaches must be taken in the second half.

Are you ready to make the game adjustments I just listed above or has fear gripped you so much that you don't want to do *anything* different? Isn't it amazing that we want more but we won't do what it takes to get more? We fantasize about living a different life but we don't believe it can really happen. This book, this game plan, this implementation after halftime is going to allow you to do just that. See, once you have the new information I'm giving you there are no more excuses. As a player, when a coach shares the halftime changes, when you go back out, it's time for you to execute the new plan. You have faith in the plan because you have faith in the deliverer of the plan. You go out and work as hard at the new plan as you did the old one. Give your first half effort to part two of your life and watch what happens. Watch how the momentum changes and live in expectation of a better outcome at the end of the game. Actively, faithfully, and conscientiously implement a new game plan. The buzzer just rang, it's time to go back in.

3RD QUARTER

2ND HALF SKILL #4

MASTERING THE "FUN"damentals

9

No Glitz or Glory, Just Gain

The fourth skill to living a better post-sports life is practicing the "Fun"-damentals. Finding the fun ...the good in everything. As athletes, the foundation of being successful in the things we want to do is doing the fundamentals. Repetition; practicing a move, a jump, a layup, a block, a tackle, a running pattern over and over and over again. We have to be willing to do the fundamentals. What's the downside to fundamentals? It's boring. Its monotonous. It's not fun. There's no ESPN for the fundamentals. There's no Twitter for the fundamentals.

The reality of it is that the fundamentals are necessary to go forward and keep growing. No matter what sport you're in you have to get the fundamentals down, you have to get the basics down or you won't advance in your play, or worse yet, you'll be extra prone to injuries. The truth is that repetition of the fundamentals makes you a better player. As much as we detest the fundamentals for the most part as an athlete, we realize the value in doing them. So the good part is that I've got to find the good in everything and fundamentals are good. So if I'm willing to embrace what's not enthusiastically fun, motivational or inspirational, those things that don't make me feel good—the fundamentals—and instead engage in the practice of doing what's necessary and finding the good in everything is what moves you through successfully. When you go out as an athlete and shoot a thousand jump shots, and dribble for hours, that's not fun, and as I said, it's boring, it's monotonous, but you have to do it unless you're committed to be a very nominal player or not playing at all. Engaging in fundamentals gets you to the next level. Most of the athletes who excel in the sports world, no matter what sport, find a way to make the fundamentals fun. They find the good in it. They're always looking at the bigger picture. They're looking down the road and using the fundamentals as a directional compass to get to where they need to be.

In sports, nobody likes to run hills. NFL players don't like doing OTA's (organized team activities). Booooring. You moan, "I don't want to go to two-a-days tomorrow. I don't want to go lift weights right now." The ones who succeed are the ones who master the fundamentals and if you take the same mindset about mastering the fundamentals when you transition out of sports, you'll go a whole lot further than others who are unwilling to do the boring basics. Just like OTA's, you don't want to go to that financial seminar, you don't want to read that business book, you don't want to listen to that podcast or webinar, you don't want to attend the mastermind group; after all, it's on the same night as the game. In the latter half, you've still got to do the boring, necessary stuff. The stuff you don't want to do.

I remember Jerry Rice who's arguably the greatest wide receiver of all time, would train in the off-season and guys would come train with him and walk away saying, "Hey, I'm not training with Jerry anymore." Walter Payton—same work ethic. His teammates would say, "What is wrong with this man?" But his work ethic was why he was never hurt, it's why he played consistently. Both Jerry and Walter mastered the fundamentals. They were willing to do all the things everyone else didn't want to do. Peyton Manning spent hours upon hours studying film. If you talk to successful people outside of sports it's the same… they do what no one else is willing to do. Personally, I get up at three or four in the morning. I've accomplished more by seven a.m. than most people do in an entire day. I'll keep working; I'll try this and try that and if something doesn't work, I'll try again a different way. Eric Thomas, the Hip Hop Preacher and Tony Robbins are great motivators but what happens is that you listen to them and you jump up to do an action but because you don't know why you're doing it, it doesn't last. Eric and Tony may get you hyped up but they don't tell the whole story. They encourage you to fight through the struggle, to fight past the pain but they don't tell you why or how so your conscious mind is activated but not your subconscious.

What athletes don't realize is that they use far more of their subconscious mind than they think. Athletes have been taught to visualize themselves running, making that kick, making that basket, blocking that play. That's all training in your subconscious.

Jack Canfield once gave an illustration of *95 horses* and how the conscious and subconscious mind works. He likened it to two sets of horses running against each other. Imagine you have ninety five horses pulling one way and five horses pulling the opposite way. He asks, "Which set of horses are going to win every time?" Obviously the ninety five horses. Here's the problem: every motivational seminar and church service only focuses on the five horses. Neither one teaches *how* to focus on the ninety five horses. We're never been taught to adjust so what I'm teaching you is *how* to adjust to the ninety five horses. The Bible says, "As a man thinks in his heart so is he." The heart and the head are connected but thoughts don't control the heart, the heart controls the thoughts. My thought life is based on how I feel. I don't think myself into a feeling, I have a feeling and then I have a thought. If you don't fix how you feel about things you can't sustain any change. That's why I'm drilling into your brain about mastering the fundamentals. When you don't understand how your brain works you can't do anything. Einstein's quote is worth repeating, "You can't fix a problem with the same mind that created it." The Bible says, "Be not conformed to this world but be transformed..." by what? By the renewing of your mind! So when you're mastering the fundamentals you must master the way you think. You've got to think differently. Dr. Caroline Leaf, author of <u>Switch On Your Brain: The Key to Peak Happiness, Thinking, and Health</u> says, "You cannot sit back and wait to be happy and healthy and have a great thought life; you have to make the choice to make this happen. You have to choose to get rid of the toxic and get back in alignment with God. You can be overwhelmed by every small setback in life, or you can be energized by the possibilities they bring." For me, the reason I didn't go to law school is because I didn't want to read anymore. When I was a kid I wanted to be an entrepreneur but there was no one in my family who was an entrepreneur so I ruled it out. In my heart and mind I picked a profession that would pay well and I like talking so I figured I'd be an attorney. Well, law school required reading a massive amount of books and I was done reading. I wasn't willing to do the monotonous, the mundane and my heart wasn't all in.

During the time I was homeless in 1988 is when I gave my life to Christ and I began to read. At the time I was introduced to some people who were in the Amway Corporation and one thing about Amway was that they had something called Standing Order and when you won that position you won book of the month and tape of the month; the people I was around had been in Amway for a while so they had books and tapes galore. I started to read and listen to motivational material. I was ingrained in the old philosophy of *focus on what you want, develop a plan, and execute that plan* so that time in my life was the beginning of a mental shift but I still found myself not having anything. I became hard-nosed passionate about the next chapters in my life because it was always in me to work hard, to go harder, to press with everything in me because of that competitive nature inside me—I just had to be better than you. As long as I worked harder than you, fine. You weren't going to beat me. That's all there was to it. I remember kids would come into Clemson wanting to take my spot and I would tell them they were going to sit on the bench. I wasn't motivated. I was competitive.

Back then motivation meant I would do something without someone telling me to do it. If you ran a mile, I would run a mile. Not a mile and a quarter, just a mile. Because all things being equal I was going to beat your butt. You do five push-ups. I'd do five. I didn't have to do more than you, I just had to keep up with you. When it came down to executing, I was going to take a dive on the court that I knew you wouldn't, I was going to take a charge I knew you wouldn't take. I was willing to do whatever it took to win but I wasn't going to put myself in a position to win because that would take extra effort but because I was competitive I relied on that. If you did more, I'd do more.

There's an old saying, "If you want to hide something put it in a book." During my Amway days when I started reading I began to do the things I didn't want to do, the little things, the mundane things. In my playing days I'd get up earlier than everybody else and I'd stay later than everybody else. I'd weight train when the other guys were out eating burgers and pizza. I'd read when they wouldn't read. So here's what I'm talking about: if you want to change your body, you have got to do the things that most people don't do. You have to get up early and exercise. You have to change the way you eat. You have to drink water. In other words, you must master the fundamentals. If you want to be successful in business you must be adept at reading and gaining the right information that will take your business forward. If you're not willing to actively engage in the fundamentals, then the ninety five horses I told you about in the 2nd Quarter are going to take you back the other way every single time.

The more you master the fundamentals the more your intelligence and emotion quotients rise. All these nuggets you are learning are an integral part of growing your mind. I'm getting you to see that your mind is the strongest tool you have. You can use what you've already been using to strengthen your mind, to show you how to cross over and keep your mind strong. Let's go back to the ninety five horses analogy. Athletes tend to live in the five percent because that's where they're accustomed to dwelling—their lives are all about getting it done. Their natural giftings and preparation are the ninety five horses. When their gifting is gone and they don't understand the ninety five horses, they're lost because that five percent is not enough to keep them going. Once you exit your sport, life is all about doing all the stuff you don't want to do—aka fundamentals. Every job you don't want to take right now, you have to take. Every book you don't want to read right now, you have to read. Whatever it is you don't want to go through right now, you must, and that includes selling the sixteen cars you never should have bought because now you need that cash.

I can always tell when athletes aren't transitioning well because I see what happens to them physically when they leave the sport. They gain weight. They get out of shape. They've quickly forgotten about the fundamentals that got them to the pinnacle of the game. Now their challenge is to master the fundamentals of eating and nutrition without a registered dietician at their beck and call. Dude, you can't throw down those five donuts anymore. Another challenge is having the unsupervised discipline to hit the weights regularly instead of sitting and exercising your fingers on the TV remote or gaming system. Who do you want to be going forward? Here's what you need to be that person:

If a player comes to me and says, "Yeah, man, I did all that discipline stuff for so long, I'm just tired of all that and I just want to let loose for a while." And their intention *is* to let loose for *a while* but they often don't ever get back into the disciplined life they had as an athlete. I tell them, "You go loosen up for a while and let's meet again in six months so you can tell me how that mindset is working for you." More often than not, they come back to me out of shape, lazy, and unmotivated. I give them a reality check about about choices and I talk to them about what their results are going to be. I never tell them what to do because that doesn't work. See what I'm saying? Actions equal results. Period. I never talk about consequences because the word alone has a negative connotation attached to it. I do tell transitioning and former players, "Everything you do is going to have an outcome whether positive or negative. The choice is yours. If you want more positive outcomes, make better choices. If you want fewer positive outcomes, make fewer positive choices. It's as simple and as difficult as that. If you don't know or understand what a positive choice is, we can talk about that, but I believe if I asked you about a choice you just made and you hem hawed, then you know. We don't have to go to school to learn how to do bad stuff. Little kids naturally lie; you don't have to teach them. Athletes who are transitioning must realize that the process is almost as if they're reverting back to being a little kid again so they literally have to start over although they're starting over with a better, stronger foundation—you're starting over with some new ideas and some fresh data. You've had success in this area of starting over because you've been traded or transferred from team to team; you just don't understand how much of what you've experienced can be utilized in your new life.

In the original Karate Kid movie, Daniel San didn't know he had documentation in the fence because he was painting fences and waxing cars and sanding the deck. He didn't know what he possessed until he had to use it. Once the lightbulb went on he realized *Oh, I do know this already. I'm already doing this but I didn't know because you didn't tell me that's what I was doing.* Attention athletes! This concept, this principle, is the whole point of this book—you already know what to do, you already have the tools, you already have the skills to be successful outside of sports. It doesn't look like what you were doing before. You are already "painting the fence, waxing the car, sanding the deck." I hope you're having an ah-ha moment. A lightbulb moment. Think about the same thing happening in the military. A lot of air force pilots exit the military and become commercial pilots. They already know how to fly a plane; they're taking their existing skill set and using it in a different way. A plan is a plane is a plane so that pilot can simply take their existing skills and learn how to fly a different type of plane—instead of flying a fighter plane, they fly a commercial plane. The lesson here is if you learn to apply what you're already doing, there's money to be made in whatever it is you want to do. If someone has been fixing cars or detailing cars in the military, they can do the exact same thing outside the military. And I don't mean working for some car company...

get creative and start your own business as a mobile mechanic or detailer. If you were my coaching client, I'd help you look at ways you can continue to do what you're doing IF it's something you love and enjoy doing.

The same principle goes for developing a greater intimacy with God. It comes down to asking yourself how much time you are spending in prayer and reading the Bible and talking to God. If you desire greater intimacy with your spouse yet you never talk to them or spend any significant time with them, then I can predict your results. This is why formula-driven ways do not work in the long run.

It's not that deep, people. I'm stating the obvious. Does this make sense to you? Take basketball for example. It is still the same game. You put the ball in the basket. You stop someone from putting the ball in the basket. That's all it is. It's still pick and roll. Football is still scoring touchdowns and blocking the other team from scoring touchdowns.

I was recently watching a documentary about the legendary Quincy Jones. He made the comment that all music, no matter what genre, is comprised of only twelve keys. When Quincy went overseas to study with the great orchestra leaders there was always ever only those twelve keys. So you've got the great classical composers like Bach and Beethoven and Chopin who have created major scores with those same twelve keys. The amount of instruments in a symphony is massive all while playing a combination of just those twelve keys. Even with all the fancy musical equipment nowadays, it still comes down to the fact that the same twelve keys are in play, however sophisticated it sounds. Quincy Jones knew how to master the fundamentals. He was Frank Sinatra's orchestra leader as a young man. He was playing trumpet for Count Basie at fourteen-years-old. Quincy and Ray Charles first met when they were fourteen- and sixteen-years-old and that's when he started writing songs for Ray Charles. He put scores together… with those same twelve notes. Is it starting to sink in now? Master the fundamentals—you already possess them.

10

Find the Good!

During part two of this thing called life, it's imperative to find the good in everything. You may ask, "What do you mean Coach Marshall?" Well, you gotta find the good at the end of your sports career. You gotta find the good in moving forward. You gotta find the good in not being in the limelight. You gotta find the good in what is and what is not! You already know how to do this because you had to find the good when you lost a game. You had to find the good in missing a shot. You had to find the good in every aspect and challenge that you faced in the first half. To have a post-sports life that grants you the success you're looking for, you must be willing to find the good in everything. All it takes is a shift in your paradigm—doing the same things within a different framework. Again, think about Daniel San in *Karate Kid*.

Reprogramming your subconscious is a necessary requirement. In order to find the good in everything, you have to begin to apply some foundational principles into your life. But before we get into that, the first thing I want you to remember is that five is the number of grace and I'll show you in a moment why that is important. New York Times bestselling author Don Miguel Ruiz published a book in 1997 called *The Four Agreements* that has sold over nine million copies. Since his first book, he has published a second book with his son, Don Jose Ruiz, called *The Fifth Agreement – A Practical Guide to Self-Mastery*. When you look at the Five Agreements and what they represent (look them up online right now so you know what I'm talking about), you'll see a way to find the good in everything. These are the Agreements you need to apply to your life so you can understand your purpose and live on a higher plane of self-awareness—then your part two will explode with greatness. I find it interesting that Don Miguel Ruiz uses five agreements because five is the number of grace. When I think of applying something to my life I think of a Band-Aid—when you apply it, it sticks. When you study and absorb what I'm telling you in the book and you apply the five agreements, that fresh knowledge begins to stick. The first of the five agreements is <u>be impeccable with your words.</u> It's important for you to speak the right things. To begin to move your thoughts in the right direction you've got to speak the right things. The word "peccable" comes from the Latin word Peccatus which means *sin*. "I'm" is a prefix which means *without*. Sin, by definition, means anything against yourself. So in order for you to truly begin to find the good in everything, you've got to be open to doing what's right for yourself and that's why the very first thing you do is to begin to speak the right things into your life. Ruiz's second agreement states <u>I can't take anything personally</u>. As athletes, we are conditioned to not take anything personally but once we're outside that element we tend to shift into taking things personally. No matter what somebody says about your new decisions, about the direction you're going, about the things you've done, the things you're currently doing, you can't take it personally. Agreement three says <u>don't make assumptions</u>. In sports we can never make assumptions. I didn't worry about assumptions because when I was told what to do during practice, and I did them, I knew I would get the results I and everyone else wanted. Second half—same thing applies. Make no assumptions about where I can be or where I'm going. I've gotta be willing to ask questions and get to the right information. Just like I did as an athlete, I'm getting the requirements for the fundamentals. I've got to *not* assume I know everything; I've got to *not* assume that my instinct will carry me, and I've got to understand that my life going forward must consist of a different kind of intelligence. The fourth agreement is <u>Always Do Your Best</u>. As an athlete, you live by this code because if you don't, you won't play for very long, or at all. Every time you go out there on the field or court you're driven to do your best. The fifth agreement is <u>Be Skeptical But Learn To Listen</u>. This agreement proves why God gave us two ears and one mouth—because listening is twice as important as running our mouth. Ruiz tells us to question everything because most of what you hear isn't true anyway. Ruiz's words still ring true, "*Be skeptical* is masterful because it uses the power of doubt to discern the truth." When we listen, we learn people's stories and we find out most of what they say is about themselves, not us. If you've been reading and absorbing this material, how do you live a victorious part two of life? By embracing these agreements. Speaking the right stuff, not taking things personally, not assuming anything, always doing our best, and learning to listen. These are the fundamentals and all you have to do is tweak them just a little to make the agreements applicable to part two of your life.

As an athlete your transition should be successful because the small tweaks, the minor game adjustments, don't take a lot—they don't take a major overhaul. Why? I'll say it again… Because you're ALREADY doing them. Now that you are aware, now that you're metacognitive, now that you understand how you think and what this transition means and the effectiveness it's going to have in your life, you'll be able to find the good in everything as you continue with the fundamentals. Find the good in everything and you'll have mastered the "Fun"damentals.

4TH QUARTER

2ND HALF SKILL #5

BUILDING A LASTING BRAND

11

Be the Brand

You are your own best brand representative! It's not your PR person or your marketing guru. It's YOU! When you play sports, your brand consisted of your athletic prowess and what you accomplished on the field or court. Building a lasting brand is about redefining who you are. Most athletes think their sports accomplishment IS their brand and it's not. In part two of your life you have to rebrand yourself just as a major corporation would and as any company will tell you, there's a lot that goes into your brand power.

Building a lasting brand has everything to do with networking while you're still playing and having a vision long before your playing days end. And, yes, your brand consists of having an exit strategy. What you have to understand is this: you as an individual *are* a brand so you have to treat yourself as a business as Adonal Foyle, former ten-year Golden State Warriors player, says in his book, *The Athlete CEO*. This whole branding machine is part of what I talk to high school athletes about. I tell them the new era of high school sports exposes young athletes to business transactions and dealings early on. In today's sports landscape, kids are playing at three or four different high schools because they're working to gain the most exposure so they go to one school one year and another school the next year. These young athletes are entrepreneurs complete with 1099's. If that's what you're going to do, you need to understand business and not simply rely on your parents or other people around you to manage your life.

One thing I tell parents, "These days your kids are being asked to choose what sport they're going to play by the time they're ten-years-old so you had better teach them how to handle themselves." If a kid has shown athletic talent and is on what William Rhoden in his book *Forty Million Dollar Slaves* calls the conveyor belt, that kid has taken everything else off the table and has all their eggs in one basket. He hasn't even thought of a Plan B because he doesn't believe it is necessary. He is certain Plan A is going to work long-term. I can tell you with one hundred percent accuracy: Plan A is never going to work long-term. But, if you follow Plan A, you will find yourself in a multi-million dollar business called sports and now you're an employee of that sport. That's why scouts, coaches and recruiting companies who don't have your best interest at heart, can come in and easily sway you into doing what is best for them and not for you. I need you to understand that when you're building a lasting brand you need to know how to take full inventory of your "business" and you need to know how to run all aspects of your business. I'll say it again if you missed it: if you want to build a lasting brand you have to start treating your life as a business.

THE ANSWER AFTER SPORTS

One aspect of a lasting brand means you absolutely positively must be more aware of what you're putting out on social media. Don't get into debates or ugly arguments with online bullies and those who seek to incite you to lose your cool. And, also, you may think you are innocently flirting with a diva with long lashes and a dynamite smile but you have to take into account that you don't really know her or her motives. Remember Luiz's words, question everything. There are so many things you will need to become aware of within your brand. A company's brand has got to include someone who is likeable because nobody wants to be part of a brand that no one likes. There has to be something about the brand that's appealing to you. What's appealing about *you*? What are people buying into? Look at Shaquille O'Neal as a brand. Look at Peyton Manning as a brand. Look at what they're doing after sports. They're making more money than they ever did in sports. Shaq has never cashed a game check; he lives off endorsements. Roger Federer was one of the greatest tennis players of all time. In 2018 Roger made nine million dollars playing tennis, making him the highest paid tennis player in history. Roger makes something close to ninety million in endorsements because he's a brand. A recent story in Forbes[2] that featured the 2019 Top 100 highest paid athletes ranked soccer great Lionel Messi as #1 followed by Roger Federer at #5, LeBron James at #8, followed by Steph Curry at #9 and Kevin Durant at #10. These guys are being asked to represent companies because they're a likeable brand. Conversely, a bunch of

---

2 Badenhausen, Kurt, The World's Highest Paid Athletes, Forbes.com, https://www.forbes.com/athletes/#3f86238c55ae (retrieved 9/18/2019)

athletes are out there who are not making money away from their sport because they are not a brand anyone wants to follow. They're not likeable. If you're not likeable as an athlete, chances are you won't be likeable after you're done playing. That means don't diss the kid in the store who asks for your autograph and to take a picture with you and you're on your cell phone the whole time. That kid is going to remember that most likely forever and he's going to tell all his friends about his experience with you. That's not the way to build a lasting brand. Deshaun Watson out of Clemson is a likeable guy. Everybody loves D-Y. He's just that dude. He'll always make money. Charles Barkley is a brand whether you agree with his opinions or not. He's charismatic. He's jovial. He's built a brand empire. He's not the sexiest dude in the world but when you're likeable you become a brand and people will look for you. Tim Tebow will make more money out of sports than he'll ever make in sports because of who he is and how he carries himself as a brand.

If a guy, say a quarterback, comes to me saying, "Hey, I don't have all that charisma these other dudes have, I'm a quiet guy so I can't build the kind of brand you're talking about because I'm not like that." I'll answer by asking them, "What sport did you play? How did you play that sport? You had to be likeable enough for your team to follow you." Brand power doesn't always mean you have to have charisma. It means your attributes and qualities must be such that others want to emulate. That was part of the reason I was so successful at Clemson and why I'm still loved by so many at Clemson—I signed those autographs. Nike decided to take a risk on former 49ers quarterback Colin Kaepernick but Nike did that for Nike. Phil Knight knows controversy sells.

How do you build a lasting brand? You build a brand that people buy into, who wants to become a part of the lifestyle that brand represents. Brands are prestigious, a cut above. You have to conduct yourself the same way, without arrogance and egotism, because there are plenty of competitors in the market that are just waiting to replace you. Think about fast food brands. You've got Burger King, McDonald's, Wendy's Chick-Fil-A; all these chains can be on the same block, even right next to each other, and they all make money. Why? Because each one has a brand concept that makes sense, that people understand. They just chose nuances that are different. One's got flame broiled, one's got fried. One's got tater tots, one's got waffle fries. They've all got a concept that works.

Sports is a concept everyone understands. When you build a personal brand that says *there's no controversy here*, it's safe for a company to put you out there. You build a lasting brand by building a better character. Developing who you are. Knowing who you are. For example, take athletes who become movie actors. They're not actors, they're entertainers because they perform in front of people so all they're doing in a movie is performing in front of people just like they did on the field or court. If you're willing to get on the stage with twenty thousand plus fans watching and cheering while you play a game, the movie set isn't going to scare you. Know your worth and just be you—I'm telling you, that's the best brand builder you'll find! You can be taught voice inflection, facial expressions and body language so you don't have to be outgoing if you want to be an actor. If you're telling me you can't be successful because you don't have a charismatic personality, all I'm hearing is an excuse.

Building a lasting brand entails considering what you are giving back, what are you leaving for others? Having a lasting brand means that you have a responsibility to give back; to your neighborhood, to your family, even to the world. Money could be used to fund reading programs, prison transition programs, at-risk youth mentoring programs, financial wellness programs, nutritional education programs, youth and adult entrepreneur programs; you name it. Most athletes are encouraged to set up foundations and most of the people running them are family so the athlete can pay them.

What I suggest you do is pool your resources together with other athletes and do something civic. One thing I thought about when Colin Kaepernick led the open field protesting is that you can't play the game your way, you've got to play the game the way it's played. You're an employee of your franchise. They control you. If what you're doing doesn't jive with their brand, they're going to tell you to stop. Try this on for size; there are thirty-two NFL teams, fifty-seven players on a team. If every player gave $100,000 you would have millions and millions of tax-deductible dollars to place in a non-profit. Now you have a pool of money and here's what I'd do with that money: hire five of the top attorneys in the country, an African-American, Hispanic, Caucasian, Jewish, and one other race, and when a racial attack by a law enforcement officer happens in a city I would deploy all my attorneys to that city. I would tell them to find out everything they can about that cop, use the pooled money and do a social media blast on him. Tell that cop, "We are going to put all your dirty laundry on every billboard in town because under our first amendment rights we have a legal right to do that." How many police officers are going to want to violate someone else's civil rights if they know a powerhouse of attorneys will come after them? What if the attorneys told the cop, "We're going to aggressively go through your books, your tax returns, and find every speck of dust and then put you on blast. You'll start seeing yourself on billboards around the city you work in and you'll be a public spectacle and disgrace." When that cop pulls someone over, they're going to be a whole lot nicer. Start fighting them with money. Start fighting where the battle is. Put the money in the media.

African-American Trailblazers with Strong Brands

When we look at what the successful rappers did early on, Dre, JayZ, and all the others, they understood that the money wasn't in front of the mic, the money was behind the mic; the money is in the production, in putting out artists, so they started their own record labels. When I look back at Sam Cooke and other jazz greats, they started their own labels. As big as their talent was, they realized the money was in the distribution.

    I tell athletes all the time, "You guys want to make money the top stars make. Why don't you want to be the one who writes the check?" We never talk about that because that's not who we see in the media. Nobody sees Arthur Blanks in the media. Nobody knows the owner of the Celtics or Milwaukee

Bucks unless you're Jerry Jones, Mark Cuban, or Robert Kraft. Nobody cares. Nobody comes to see the owner. Players have a game shelf life of two to three years in the NFL, four to six years in the NBA. Yet ownership is generational. Look at Stephen Jones, Jerry's son. The good ol boy network is hard to get in, no question, yet in the history of the world, once African-Americans found a way to get into an industry, they found a way to change the game. Take Arthur Ashe, Althea Gibson, Jesse Owens and Tiger Woods, for examples. When Tiger started swinging that club he represented everything that wasn't golf. He didn't represent an aristocratic population nor anyone with a stuffy up-in-the-air nose. He was a black dude playing in a white sport and he dominated their whole world. Basketball wasn't a sport that was originally meant for African-Americans but you let us in and look what happened. The Tuskegee Airmen is another great example. We weren't allowed in but once we got a chance to prove ourselves we were the best combat pilots the world had ever seen. The business world wasn't necessarily meant for African-Americans either but again, once we get in, we dominate because we've been through wins and losses, we've been through change in management, we've been through severe adversity. Back in the day there were no African-American quarterbacks because team ownership didn't think we were smart enough to play the position. But then in 1968 Marlin Briscoe became the first starting African-American quarterback in the American Football League after being drafted by the Denver Broncos, and established a Denver rookie record of fourteen touchdown passes his first season. After racism ended his career as a passer, Briscoe reinvented himself as a Pro Bowl wide receiver. He was a pioneer, a trailblazer and we're well aware of the great African-American quarterbacks who followed his footsteps. Of course the history of African-Americans in the NFL precedes Briscoe. Fritz Pollard and Bobby Marshall were the first African-American players in the NFL in 1920, and Pollard, the first African-American head coach in the NFL. Michael Vick changed how the quarterback position was played. I'm still trying to figure out why African-Americans don't play soccer and volleyball at a high level in America. I believe the reason lies somewhere in the fact that there's not a documented history to follow. When I look at sports I can look back at baseball's history I find Jackie Robinson and Satchel Page, and before them, Moses Fleetwood Walker (1856 – 1924). I can find documented success in basketball during the Harlem Renaissance. I can find documented success in football when I look at Jim Brown. The ones who paved the way, yet I can't find documented history of African-American involvement in volleyball or soccer.

No Excuses

With such iconic examples of what is possible, today's players have no excuse as to why they can't excel in any arena inside or outside of sports. Everything you will go through in business you've already been through in sports; coach got fired, roster changes, general team climate changes, teammate dynamics, good days and bad days. Are you starting to make the connection? You've already been prepared for your second half!

You've been groomed for this since Little League and if you decide business is what you're going to do in your post-sports career, the contacts you have access to during your playing days and how you leverage those contacts will open wide the doors. Bernie Kosar, former player for the Cleveland Browns and one of my good friends, we had a company called Euphoria. It's one of the only companies in the world that customizes nutritional supplements based on a person's DNA. Bernie wanted to do an event in Cleveland so we got the word out that Bernie was going to be there and there were six, maybe seven hundred people in that room over two nights. If you have that type of pull and leverage with people, and you do, if you have products and services, the public would rather support you than the average Joe on the corner. If you open a restaurant, people would rather come to your restaurant because it has your name attached to it. Most every guest hopes they might run into you, or that you will come to their table and ask how their meal was. You were their favorite player and now they're going to eat at your establishment.

The question often comes up with icons like Dre and JayZ of why aren't these guys buying sports teams. I think the answer lies in the fact that there still exists a plantation mentality that says I'll let you coach the slaves, not own slaves. I believe there's still residue in the African-American culture of collaboration and not getting along; I'll get mine and you get yours type of mentality. When you look at other cultures, they'll collaborate. Most record companies are owned by Jewish people. Hollywood is another example. Jewish people come from a philosophy of pooling their resources and doing things together and everybody shares in the wealth—they operate in an abundance mentality unlike African-Americans who often operate in a scarcity mentality especially since we came from nothing. A lot of athletes don't mind going back to nothing because it's familiar.

The good thing is that former players are starting to buy into the ownership concept. Derek Jeter is leading the ownership group with the Florida Marlins. Magic Johnson is part of the ownership group for the Dodgers. Usher acquired part ownership of the Cleveland Cavaliers. Michael Jordan has a large majority ownership of the Charlotte Hornets. There are also a select group of African-American guys out there who have minority ownership in investment groups who own various teams although there are still not many who are in the forefront, and I don't believe it will happen until we have a vested belief in camaraderie and working together. Again, there's no documented history so it's a matter of who's going to be the first. Former president Barack Obama serves as an example; regardless of your political affiliation, he served in the only position in the world that no one ever thought you'd see an African-American. Documented history in action. He was Harvard Law and was groomed the right way. He had the look; clean cut, married, articulate, charismatic and young enough to still be embraced by all. The Obamas were a hip couple. Fun. He played basketball, Michelle wasn't afraid to get out there and have fun with the public. They were, together, an immensely strong brand. They still are.

My point in talking about all this is to show you how important a strong brand is. I've talked a lot about the African-American brand but whether you're Black, White, Hispanic, Asian, Indian, or whatever, you are responsible for building your own brand and to be a trailblazer in whatever you do. A disruptor which means you observe what everyone else is doing and then do something different. You can enlist the help of a brand building group but it's ultimately up to you. Just remember, your brand is how you live your life in public and private so make it count.

12

The After Party – What Does YOUR Brand Look Like?

As the discussion continues in this chapter on how to build a lasting brand, you will come to fully understand that your personal brand and how it looks, smells, feels, and is perceived by others, is expected of an individual when they elevate themselves in the arena of sports. But when we make our transition, it's even more important in the arena of our everyday lives. Because most of us are going to be remembered for what we did after sports is over as opposed to what we did when we played. When you think about the thousands of players to ever play the game of football and basketball, there are really only a select few who have high level notoriety and successful years of playing in the professional ranks. For the NFL, the average career is three years and for the NBA it's four to five years. So building a brand is critical in how your part two plays out. While you're playing, your brand is being developed and it allows you to present yourself uniquely in the marketplace. Your brand allows you to garner a following, especially on social media platforms. There's not an athlete in the world, doesn't matter what level they are, who doesn't have a Twitter account, or a Facebook or Instagram account, and maybe even LinkedIn. What used to be a silent building of your brand now becomes an open and exposed building of your brand. Most don't realize the impact their brand has until something extremely negative happens, or there's a misperception of who you really are based on what's been shown through your social media.

I believe there are five things you need to do to build a lasting brand. Did you notice that number five popping up again? Remember, five is the number of grace. When we study it from a biblical standpoint, grace is the ability to bounce back and that means that building a strong brand requires grace because you're essentially "bouncing back" from your sports career into a new chapter in your life. The following are five critical brand-building points I want to share with you.

1. Give in value what you're willing to take in payment. When you were an athlete, whether that payment was a scholarship, something you received at the high school level, or any monetary gift, if you were able to go to the professional level, you were expected to give a certain amount to receive the payment. In part two of your life, you've got to give in value what you're willing to take in payment. When you step off of that platform and pedestal of the demand that is created by the sports world, you have got to find the next thing to do and in doing that you have to find a way that you're willing to give in value what you are willing to take in payment. You've got to under promise and over deliver. What are you willing to give in value? That will justify what you get in payment. You have to move from that entitlement mentality that you experienced as an athlete—stuff was given to you because you had athletic talent. Giving in value what you get in payment is the first thing you need to do to build a strong, lasting brand. The information you are receiving here serves as the headlights, the high beam, to navigate your brand successfully.

2. **Understand that your income will be determined by the many people you serve and how well you serve them**. In the sports world you're serving a lot of people—from an entertainment standpoint, from a fan standpoint, and you get paid accordingly. The more people you entertain, the more people who love what you do, the greater your compensation. Understand this—in your post-sports life your income will be determined by how many people you serve and how well you serve them. As I just said, you did this as an athlete, you served the team owners, the team, and the fans by displaying your talent, by playing at the highest level, giving your all. People bought tickets to see you, they followed you on Instagram, they talked about you and your ability. Now it's about serving people in a different capacity. This shift isn't a giant shift because you've done it all along.

3. **You need to place others' interests before your own**. In order to build a better brand you've got to put other people first. If you're in a team-based atmosphere, you usually are able to engage with other teammates because it's the collective group that makes the greater good. However, sometimes in the sports world we tend to be arrogant, egotistical and

self-centered and that mindset is definitely one that requires a shift if you want a phenomenal part two. It's not like you didn't have to keep yourself in check at some point in your athletic career, or maybe a coach kept you in check. How you managed to take your ego down a notch and how you were able to keep it under control is an individual matter. In your part two you're going to have abundantly put others interest before yours.

4. Understanding that the most valuable gift you give to others is yourself. You gotta be you and you gotta be real. As an athlete that's what defined you, that was what drew people to you. It was what made them want to like you, whether you were a good guy or a bad guy. It's peculiar because the bad boys are revered and respected in the sports world. Again, in your post-sports life, you simply have to make a minor tweak, but you must be authentic. Most athletes at the core of who they are respect their God-given ability, they respect the people with whom they engage. Usually, when you get an athlete away from the sport you get to touch the real person who's down to earth, real, and a normal guy who's all about having a good time. Most athletes want their part two life to reflect who they really are and they want to blend in like just another guy. The most valuable gift you can give somebody else is who you really are. Because when the bright lights are gone people get to know the real you. There is story after story of athletes who give back, who have big hearts, and who show their authenticity because it truly defines who they were all along, even though the bright lights can blind us for a moment to who we really are.

5. In this new shift of giving, you have to be open to receiving. Most athletes are constantly asked to give. They're asked to give their time, their resources, and their money. But in this new era, you have to be open to receiving. There are people out there who aren't out to take everything from you, manipulate you, or use you. There are people out there who genuinely will put away the things you did as an athlete and meet you at your new level. But you have to be open to it. It's a hard shift for some athletes because they're so used to being in control. Being willing to receive isn't giving up control, it's allowing other critical pieces and people in your life to come and sow into you and give to you to fortify you, just like you needed as a team. I was a point guard so I needed the 2, the 3, the 4 and the 5 to make me the best point guard I could be. A quarterback needs the offensive line, the wide receivers, the tight ends, the running backs, and the defense to make him the person he needs to be. A golfer needs his caddy. A tennis player needs his coach. All these things are a part of what's necessary and you have to be willing to accept their input if you want to win.

Again, these are things done in the sports world, but they're not so easily transferred outside of sports. You already have a DNA- wired success blueprint inside you that if you just took a second to rewire and recalibrate it for your post-sports life you would literally have a familiar blueprint to move you into your part two life. The building and strengthening of your brand, this paying it forward mentality, is part of what needs to be done for your second half. Even though you're entering new territory, the familiarity of execution will allow you to take what you learned in sports and apply it in the here and now. Let's summarize the five points:

1. Give in value what you expect in payment.
2. Realize your income will be based on the amount of people you serve and how well you serve them.
3. Make sure you put the interests of others before your own.
4. Remain who you are, it's the most valuable gift you can give anyone.
5. You have to be as willing to receive as you are to give.

This grace-filled plan I'm laying out for you to allow you to win big in your life after sports is something that you as an athlete should naturally flow into. This book, these platform rules, these keys, these principles, when applied, will totally shift where you are today to where you're stepping into—your future.

Coming up, we're going to look at five (there's that 5 again) indispensable keys to unlock your success. We're almost done with our journey and you've learned a lot about what it takes to really thrive in your post-sports life but this next section is really power-packed so hang on for the ride.

FINAL BUZZER

13

The 5 Indispensable Keys for Your 2nd Half

You should consider it exciting if you're struggling with this shift out of sports into the real world because the ability to do that is accompanied by grace. *"Whaaaat?"* you may be thinking right now. *"You want me to be excited about struggling?" "I don't know, man"*. Allow me to explain.

I talk to so many former athletes around the country and the same message prevails, the same stories exist—the frustrating demise of so many athletes after their sports career is over. I started my third quarter in the same place; not in the mental or emotional space I needed to be. I sought God and He gave me direction. He pressed upon my spirit to give back to people who needed it, namely my fellow athletes, but really, anyone who is in transition. He wanted me to be an influencer, a life-changer,j and a difference maker.

In this chapter I want to impress on you the five keys that revolutionized my own life and will also change yours in a powerful way as you incorporate them into your daily life.

KEY #1 – MENTAL

Let's recap the 95 horses analogy because it relates to the mental key. Jack Canfield illustrates it this way: two sets of horses are running against each other. Imagine you have ninety five horses pulling one way and five horses pulling the opposite way. He asks, "Which set of horses are going to win every time?" Obviously the ninety five horses.

What I've taught you in this book, so far, is *how* to adjust to the ninety five horses. Your mindset must shift to the 95 horses because that's where your power is. That's where your success lies. Positive daily affirmations are the 95 horses. Here are a handful to repeat daily:

Do Positive Just Because...

"It empowers me to do my best work."

"It's a gift I can give myself and others."

"It means I own my place; no excuses or complaining."

"It clears my mind and frees my spirit."

"My thoughts and feelings create my outcome."

Questions for Thought

1. How can I become more mentally accountable? (Positive affirmations? Positive self-talk? Tape a picture of a herd of horses to my bathroom mirror to remind me of the 95 horses?)

2. Am I willing to study my mental game film? (What is it showing? Who is it starring? Too many commercials? Does it reveal a reel of bloopers?)

KEY #2 – PHYSICAL

Tommy Lasorda, Hall of Fame baseball player and manager once said, *"In baseball and in business, there are three types of people; those who make it happen, those who watch it happen, and those who wonder what happened."* The physical key is mastering the FUNdamentals, doing those things you don't want to do in order to become who you really want to become. Do the mundane by spending 10 minutes a day reading a success book or personal development book.

Questions for Thought

1. Which type of person am I in the Tommy Lasorda quote? I will own my response.
2. Am I willing to study my physical game film? (Will I make a list of those things I don't want to do and start doing them and checking them off—challenge yourself by making it a personal contest.)

KEY #3 – EMOTIONAL

This crucial key is all about making it happen right where you are; living in the present moment. Yes, you're taking full accountability for what's gone wrong in the past, and, if necessary, making amends for your actions, but now your slate is clean. Work from where you are at this moment. Key #3 is also about preparing yourself emotionally for life's blitzes, which come in many forms. Some blitzes feel like knockout punches when they happen but I'm here to tell you that you WILL survive and you can even go on to share your emotional journey with others so they, too, might be encouraged.

Questions for Thought

1. Am I living in the present moment despite past mistakes?
2. Am I willing to study my emotional game film? (Some mistakes just don't go away so easily, so in what ways am I making wise amends with those I may have hurt in the past?)

KEY #4 – FINANCIAL

"It isn't the mountains ahead to climb that wear you out; it's the pebble in your shoe." Muhammad Ali, World Heavyweight Champion Boxer

This fifth key, your financial well-being, can be likened to building a lasting brand. Your financial health is not so much about what you have (or have left), it's what you're doing with what you do have. When asked how we define wealth, most people's first impression is always to say money, money, money, cars, houses, toys, and money, money, money. But wealth is so much more than all that. There are wealthy people who live in grass huts in third world countries because love is in abundance in their households. Wealth is having good health. Wealth is having family and friends who love and support you. Wealth is waking up each day with a smile on your face and a song in your heart. So, how are you leveraging your wealth in the real sense of the word? As far as money goes, yes, it sure does make life a whole lot easier and if you want to protect and provide for yourself and your family you'll need to know "the state of your flocks" (Proverbs 27:23), garner wise financial counsel and make sound decisions on where you want to be.

Questions for Thought

1. How do I define wealth?
2. Am I willing to study my financial game film? (What steps will I take today to secure my future wealth in all areas?)

KEY #5 - SPIRITUAL

Our spiritual life is all about love; having love for God, for our family and friends, for those less fortunate, and for ourselves. It's our mad love for the game that will give us the stickability to hold it together when things get tough…and it's the binder that holds our life together when things are going smoothly.

Questions for Thought

1. What is the best description of my spiritual life right now? (How much effort do I give to maintaining it?)
2. Am I willing to study my spiritual game film? (Do I need to make some game adjustments to get closer to my spiritual source?)

See what we've done? We've taken the five skills (study the film, present moment living, mad love for the game, mastering the FUNdamentals, and building a lasting brand) and applied them to the five indispensable keys: mentally, physically, emotionally, financially, and spiritually. Take each key, each skill, and put it into practice, and you WILL be successful in your second half. Focus on one at a time so it really becomes embedded in your brain, and then move on to the next one. Before long, you will start to witness amazing things happening in your life!

O.T.

(OUTTAKES)

14

Need a Coach?

When you were at the height of your success, in the best place you could possibly be athletically, working the hardest you could work, and achieving all you wanted to achieve, you had coaches. You looked for coaches, you used coaches; it was a part of what you did. You HAD to have a coach! The same thing is necessary during your part two life, in fact, it's even more important outside of sports because at least in the sports arena your skillset, natural ability, and instinct play a major role in how effective you could be.

When you get outside of what you can rely on you definitely need some instructions. What was in you during sports came out with a sports coach and now, in your second half, it's going to come out a different way with a sports transition coach or a life coach. Same skillset—different manifestation. Hopefully this makes you more aware of the type of coaching you need in your third and fourth quarters. You do need a coach who can help you transition but you don't need somebody who's going to cause you to be dependent. Seek a coach who's going to teach you and release you to:

- ☐ Identify your values and live your life by them
- ☐ Reach the pinnacle of your success
- ☐ Make choices that empower your second half
- ☐ Thrive in relationships that are mutually nurturing

I tell my clients all the time that my goal is to teach you not to need me but to be there when you do. Proverbs 18:16 says "A man's gift will make room for him and bring him before great men." If what I'm saying sparks an interest, and you want the best transition coach on the planet, feel free to visit my website at http://www.graysonmarshalljr.com.

15

Setting Goals the Right Way

I explained to you in Chapter 4 that we would re-visit the 4-step process that Alexander Lloyd spells out in his book, *Beyond Willpower*. What follows is a breakdown of his 4-step goal setting process:

1) The goal you set has to be <u>in truth</u>, meaning that it has to be something that's doable. As a young kid, when we looked at and evaluated ourselves athletically we had to set goals in truth. Muggsy Bogues and Spud Webb are a couple of the shortest players in NBA history. They both defy natural logic because Spud is 5'7" and Muggsy is 5'3". Neither were typical build for the NBA. However both of them, as well as, Earl Boykins, 5'5" and Keith Jennings, 5' 7" actually had lengthy NBA careers although they were all an anomaly. Most short guys usually end up giving up their basketball careers because it's really not in truth.

Statistically, even more far fetched than the NBA height anomaly, is that there are over 550,000 kids playing high school basketball in the world today and less than 1% make it to the pros. The numbers are just as staggering for football and baseball, so the amount of people who can get to that next level are very few. That means you may have a sports destination goal, sports dreams that are high school based, maybe college based, but that's as far as it goes. So the goal has to be in truth. We can evaluate the truth based on our athletic ability.

2) The goal has to be <u>in love</u>. The truth part of it is the "what." The love part is the "why" I am doing it. I told you before that you already have this part of it covered; you love the game. You love the world of sports. You love the access, the pageantry, everything that goes along with the sports world. When you transition out of sports you must find something to do that you love, not what you will tolerate.

3) The goal has to be <u>100% in your total healthy control</u>. When I'm working on my sport, when I'm working on my craft, it's only me. I'm out dribbling like Steph Curry, I'm out shooting like Ray Allen, I'm running, I'm lifting. It's *me* doing those things. The execution is one hundred percent in my total healthy control of my goal. It's all on me.

4) The goal has to be done <u>in the present moment</u>. The present moment means the actual engaging is right here and right now. See, the reason athletics is so successful is because you can see and measure incremental gains

as you're moving toward and progressing toward the end result you want. You're progressing forward every day, so every day you're getting better. What you're doing is in the present moment and you're seeing success—that's why it's easy to keep going. It's easier to keep striving because every day you put forth effort, you're seeing yourself getting better, stronger, more precise.

I tell people all the time, if you want to change your life tomorrow, there are two things you can do right now that will make that happen. Number one is to have no emotional connection to any outcome, and number two is set no timeframe for things to happen. We do the opposite of those two things all the time and we wonder why we don't see our goals realized. You don't set a timeframe because it's not you giving the timeframe….God delivers when He wants to deliver so you can project out thirty days all you want. If your goal lines up in thirty days, that's wonderful but if you're not ready for it, it's not coming. God does not work on our timeframe so how are you going to impose your timeframe on His plan? I fully understand that this thought process goes against status quo teaching but I say if you want status quo results, keep yourself in status quo thinking. What I'm giving you are tools to take you farther than you ever dreamed possible and it takes bucking traditional methods and making a mindset shift to some new ideas.

16

Building New Networks

Building new networks has much to do with building lasting brands. A lot of the old connections you had, and the people you met, can still provide value at the next level but you now have to surround yourself with people who are intimately knowledgeable about the new job, the *new* business, the new entrepreneurial adventure you want to do. Whatever your next endeavor looks like you have to get a new network of people. My old network most likely doesn't fit my new endeavor because they don't have experience in my new space. Your social network doesn't create a business network. Most of the time those in your athletic network are the ones who are taking from you. You've provided a lifestyle for them. What you need now is someone who can teach you what you need to move into and operate in your new endeavor. Someone YOU can plug into. Usually, you are the icon that people want to be with. Now you must become the student and that involves a new network and new information gathering. New books. New understanding. This is why I reference O.T. as Outtakes because it's about who can help you position yourself, who can pour into YOUR life. Whoever can help you, you need to serve them so that you can be in place for the law of reciprocity, the Biblical principle in Luke 6:38, "Give and it shall be given unto you, good measure, pressed down, shaken together, running over shall men give unto your bosom." Your post-sports life is about identifying and changing the emphasis from giving to receiving in your new networks. You've been accustomed to you giving and people taking. Now you're giving AND you're receiving.

Often people in your static networks like family will want to force themselves along with you into your new network. You know they're not going to serve you well in that new network yet you have to keep them to a certain extent because they're family. You must understand and maintain control of your new space. While you can't ever fully get rid of family, you know they're going to be a deterrent to your new space, a negative part of what you're doing, a distraction that hinders you from reaching your goals. If you know that to be true, then they can't be there. People and relationships equate to simple math. There are people who add to your life, who multiply your life, and people who subtract from your life, or divide your life. The only ones you need are the ones who add or multiply. That goes for everybody! That doesn't mean you don't care for them or love them but they're not significant right now for the direction and plan that you have. If you choose to have family members in your new space, they need to come alongside in the way you need them and you must be okay with telling them "This is the way it's going to be." Building new networks is defining where you're going and what you want and being able to articulate it. The more you set defining parameters around your life the better you will feel about who you are, and the easier it is to do.

17

Word Traps (Proverbs 18:21)

In the Good News Translation, Proverbs 18:21 says, "What you say can preserve life or destroy it; so you must accept the consequences of your words." I think it's very important, especially for athletes, to be particularly mindful of what you say to yourself when you're no longer in a place of confidence, when you're no longer in a place where you feel competent. When your confidence is gone it is easy to start talking to yourself in the wrong way. What you don't realize is that you're going to have to deal with what you say. For example, you might say, "Well I didn't mean that," but it doesn't matter, that's not how this whole thing works. It's not the intention of what you said, it's what *intentionally* came out of your mouth.

When you look at this principle and understand it conceptually, you place a hyphen in your life when you say things like, "I'm frustrated, I don't know what to do, I'm not in a good place, I don't know what I'm going to do next." What happens when you verbalize such things you're going to get more of exactly what you're saying. Here's what I mean so understand me clearly: when you make negative statements "the Universe" (and I'm not going to get caught up in semantics or a theological talk about God and the Universe) responds to whatever you say—it takes to heart. Imagine the Universe as a literal accepter of words so whatever you say it's going to take it as truth. The Universe doesn't know the intention, it doesn't know what you meant, it only knows what it heard. When you keep declaring, "I don't know what I'm going to do" or "I'm not equipped to do this" that's what you're going to get. It's not magic so it doesn't happen overnight but it's what you're building a foundation to accept. Your words are very powerful—how you speak about yourself, how you accept what other people say about you—because what other people say about you, you tend to repeat. We were taught as kids to read, recite, repeat, and respond. We usually mimic what someone says about us and when we're alone it becomes our thought process, and the more we verbalize it the more it becomes real. It's like writing your book according to someone else's script, thoughts and ideas. Whether or not it's the book you want, if it's the book you spoke, it's the book you're going to get.

As an athlete transitioning out of sports you've got to be careful what you say. This is a big deal! Am I asking you to be overly concerned? No! What I'm telling you is that studies have been done and the average person has fifty to sixty thousand thoughts a day and over ninety percent of those thoughts are negative. They've also found that the frequency and power of a positive thought has a thousand times greater impact than a negative thought. If you do the math, there's fifty to sixty positive thoughts and those thoughts can counteract almost every negative thought you have. When you're having negative thoughts, don't stay in that space, instead find someone to engage with about those negative thoughts. When you're following your passion and purpose, whether you're succeeding at the level you want to or not, you're constantly thinking about your progress or lack thereof. So your lack of success might not feel good but you absolutely love what you're doing and it changes your frequency to a higher level. The higher the frequency the greater the response. That's why the Bible says that "the power of life and death are in the tongue". Here are a couple of examples of word traps:

1. I don't know what I'm going to do with the rest of my life.
2. I'm not good enough to do that or be that or get that.
3. I lost all my money and I don't know what to do now.
4. I'll do it tomorrow.
5. I don't know what I'm going to do now that I'm not playing ball.

These statements might seem small in and of themselves but they're building blocks for complacency, comfort, rejection, and remorse. And it's not just about saying these things aloud to others, it's what you're internally saying to yourself. The bottom line is what you're saying is going to have an effect on you.

How can you actively reverse those word traps?

Enlist the help of a Metacognition coach like me because accountability is a big part of moving forward and the speed in which you move forward. When I work with clients, I'm constantly on them about their words. I help them reframe by telling them, "Let's not say it that way." The client might respond, "I didn't mean it that way" and I, in turn, respond, "Let's not say it that way." What happens is that the more you reframe your words, the more you become consciously aware of what is coming out of your mouth, and as a result, the more you catch yourself. Let's revisit what Einstein said, "You cannot fix a problem with the same mind that created it."

When we look at how we process information, we process it from:

- *unconscious incompetence* (I don't know what I don't know) to:
- *conscious incompetence* (I'm aware of what's going on but I don't know how to fix it) to:
- *conscious competence* (I'm aware of what's going on and I know what I need to do to fix it) to:
- *unconscious competence* (I do it without thinking).

That's how we process information. In football, you don't know if your technique for blocking is bad if you've always been able to block. All of a sudden a coach tells you what you're doing is not the best thing and shows you a better way to do it. You now realize that you can fix your technique but it may take time because you'll naturally default to what you know and the way you've been doing it. After a while of practicing a new move, a new block, a new jump shot, you finally get it and ultimately it becomes your new default. People want to do what works but I say do what's right because what's right will always work. Sometimes the wrong thing works but it's not until they feel the pain from how they're doing it that they consider a new way.

18

Confidence and Faith are Two Different Things

The reason I want you to understand the difference between confidence and faith is this: faith is the one reason you don't decide to move forward because you don't have the confidence in the new place you're going. Confidence is what carried you during your sports career and for some of you reading this, if you're honest with yourself, it was more like cockiness.

For this next part of your life you're going to need faith, "the substance of things hoped for, the evidence of things not seen." You're going to have to begin to trust like never before because you are directly involved; it's not the team owners and coaches and trainers, it's YOU. Let's say your skill was speed. In your post-sports career nobody cares how fast you ran if you're now running your own business. If your skill was strength, or you were known for your jump shooting, nobody cares. The confidence you had in your skill set is no longer applicable. Now you have to have faith that the skills God gave you were not seasonal, they were for a lifetime. If God gave you the ability to shoot baskets or run a football, then He gave you that ability for a reason, because it's going to, if you work with it, translate into something. The faith comes in knowing that you can use your skillset and then trusting the right timing will prove where that skillset needs to be. A lot of athletes fall after sports because their confidence is only in one specific area and it's relegated to what they do, not who they are. I want you to be confident in who you are as a human being, not in what you do or have done. If you'll utilize the sum of all of who you are, plus all the challenges you've faced and overcome, it's impossible for you not to be successful.

19

Greed, Ego, and Insecurity

These three things, greed, ego, and insecurity can tear any athlete down. If you don't resolve this unholy trinity as a player, it will potentially ruin you after sports is over.

Greed: If greed was an issue during your playing days, welcome to your new world: now you're no longer making the money, and we all know that companies don't give a signing bonus when they hire you. You may still have your athlete lifestyle so you may be willing to compromise who you are or what you're willing to do in order to maintain that lifestyle. If you're greedy you won't want to let all that stuff go yet I can virtually guarantee you that they will be weights around your neck as time marches forward.

Ego: You've been the guy, the showstopper, the attention-grabber for so long. Unfortunately, that's no longer going to happen because you now realize you've been a team employee who's been used and the powers-that-be don't care anymore so the reality check is: who you thought you were doesn't matter at this point. You're not running over players, you're not shooting jump shots, you're not playing hockey or soccer or whatever your sport was. It was nice when you were there, you still have your jersey but it's not the same because the franchise has quickly moved on to the next young, bright, and shiny guy. The more you think that jersey is going to mean something in your post-sports career the more you're going to find out it's not. Carrying your ego into your part two life is going to be detrimental just like when you were playing.

Insecurity: When you have been defined by what you did on the court or field for so long, you won't know who you are in your part two—you walk into a restaurant or bar or a new job and nobody recognizes you or even knows who you are, except that you're a new employee. That's a harsh reality that can often plunge you into asking, "Who am I?" This is why we have to increase our E.Q. (emotional quotient).

Not allowing greed, ego, and insecurity to rule you displays emotional intelligence and fortunately that's an area in which you can grow and learn. If you have a high level of emotional intelligence you can get over these things but if you don't and you stay in that former "I am somebody" space, that unholy trinity will continue to plague you. As an athlete your skillset is your I.Q., your talent is your elevated I.Q. but when that I.Q. is depleted your E.Q. is going to go right out the window with it. Fortunately, as I said, you can learn E.Q., and that will be your saving grace in your second half.

20

Stop Believing Your Press, Instead, Believe Your DNA

The second book I wrote, *Maintaining Greatness*, speaks of Genesis 1:26, "We're made in the image and likeness of God." We tend to forget Genesis 1:26 after we've used up our God-given ability during our sport. We must remember who we are and whose likeness we were made in as we maneuver through our post-sports career.

Press clippings give you an elevated belief in who you are as opposed to looking at your DNA. You're a child of the King and whether you believe it or not God says, "All souls are mine." Whether you acknowledge Him or not, He acknowledges you. If you really understood who you are IN HIM, your life would be a whole different story after you're done playing ball. If you were the son of someone famous, like the Queen of England, or the President of the United States, or a famous movie star, or Oprah Winfrey's child, what in the world do you think you wouldn't be able to have? You would be lacking nothing because your parent has all the resources to buy you whatever you wanted. You'd have access to places the general public would never gain access to. Let's take Oprah—understanding who she is changes who you are. If I was born and raised a Kennedy kid, I would expect to be raised a certain way. I would expect to be given some privileges and rights because I'm a Kennedy. If I was Barack Obama's child, I would be afforded opportunities just because I was his kid.

We can reflect on that in the natural but how much more does that apply to you as God's kid? God has more money and resources than anyone on this earth could ever hope to have. Oprah has money, lots of it, but it's nothing in comparison to what God has. So if you really look at your DNA, if you look at who's child you really are, why would you feel like you aren't worthy or can't have what it is you want. You have designer GENES (not jeans) because you are a child of the King of Kings. We have access to all the Father has! That's your DNA, that's your qualifier.

21

If you *are* god, why do you need a God?

Elevated appreciation and acknowledgement of men can make you a "little g" god. Social media, TV, everything, puts you in the forefront and makes you a very visible person. During your playing days it might have been easy to mistake yourself for a "little g" god. After all, you can pretty much do whatever you want with no repercussions or consequences. Most athletes after their sports career is over come to realize that they aren't a god and that they need God. We've seen it splashed across our screens when something tragic happens, an athlete will suddenly make a shift into a different way of thinking about the way he needs to live his life.

Knowing who you are comes by knowing who He says you are. Walk in your worth! Surrender being a "little g" god because God says He'll have no other gods before Him. The principles of God work whether you believe in Him or not.

22

He Didn't Give You Seasonal Ability, But Rather Lifetime Ability

Seasonal ability is utilizing your visible gift for your benefit. There's so much more inside you than what you've tapped into thus far. God gave you the ability for your season of sports yet you already possess a lifetime skillset that you may not even be aware of yet. God didn't *just* make you fast because ultimately at some point fast isn't going to serve you anymore. He gave you the skills you needed for a season to maximize and use and you must now use what He's given you for the next season. The Bible says in 1 Corinthians 13:11 "When I was a child, I spoke as a child, I understood as a child, I thought as a child; but when I became a man, I put away childish things." When I was in basketball I did basketball things, and now that I'm not in basketball I have to do other things. We must understand what that transition really looks like.

If you're thinking that all you have is what you had for sports; running, jumping, blocking, and now you don't recognize that you possess any talent or skills for your second half, you have to ask, *how is that mentality serving me?* If you ran a 4.25, tell me, what job is that skill going to work in when you're forty-two years old. I can virtually guarantee you that you won't even be able to run a 4.25 when you're forty-two. Tap into your lifetime ability—it's there inside you!

CONCLUSION

Knowing What I Know Now, What Do I Do Next?

This book project has been so exciting because it revealed some things to me in the middle of writing. The original approach I was going to take with the book was to focus more on how differently you must do things in your third and fourth quarters of life. During the course of writing the content, God showed me that you just need to do what you did in the first half in a little different way. That's such a revelatory thing to embrace because there's not as much tweaking necessary to live a successful, vibrant, purposeful post-sports life. It's just like halftime—when you go in the locker room the coach doesn't completely switch up the game plan, he simply makes a few small tweaks to get the outcome the team desires. Your second half is all about making a few halftime tweaks. Your life game is not over. Understand that this book is founded on grace so the mistakes you've made until this day are washed away and now you can live YOUR most successful second half.

About the Author

THE COACH

Grayson has the distinctive talent of "getting you to believe in you." His unique ability to highlight, isolate, and obliterate mental blocks is why people call him the "Metacognition Expert." A nationally respected influence in the basketball community, Grayson is a highly sought-after consultant for a host of college and professional teams as well as corporations.

Professionally, Grayson is well known as "The Coach of Coaches." He mentors a broad scope of C-suite executives and sports coaches to elevate their productivity and accountability. He consults with professional athletes and military and non-profit organizations to implement and maintain best practices while monetizing strategies so they can stand out in their respective markets.

THE AUTHOR

Grayson's first book *Do Positive – The Keys to the Life You Always Imagined* is a mind-shifting book that has changed countless lives as readers experience immediate changes through genuine awareness and understanding of how they think, and also learn how to put a stop to personal destructive cycles that stymie success.

His second book *Maintaining Greatness – Managing your Gifts for Limitless Living* is all about reclaiming your birthright and rightfully positioning yourself in the path of blessing. Apply the principles in this book and you will learn the importance of maintaining greatness and truly living in the power of who you were born to be.

THE ACC LEGEND

In 1988, with 857 assists, Grayson left Clemson as the All-Time assist leader and the All-Time leader in the ACC, including a single game record of 20 assists and career records of 7.02(career average) and 7.71(season). He was named Clemson's 2016 ACC Legend although Grayson admits the best part about Clemson was simply being a student and enjoying campus life. He was inducted into the Clemson Hall of Fame in 2009.

Acknowledgments

Thank you to my family, I love you always: My kids, Amber, Ciara, Tre and Devyn; and my grands, Keshaun, Keaun, Amia and Aubrey Carter (A.C.). To my deceased mother, Marie and my deceased father, Grayson, Sr. who set a foundation for me to always help and serve. To my sister, Dr. Terri Marshall who listened and understood; and most importantly, supported.

Thank you to my God-inspired team: Michelle Hill, Your Legacy Builder at Winning Proof and her team of experts, including Drew Becker of Realization Press.

Thank you to Edwinna Wilkerson (Sunshine) for her professional editing and proofreading.

Thank you to MOVMT Group & Mark Calibrone for branding and marketing. Dr. Adrian A. Gentry for cover layout and design.

I also wish to acknowledge Alexander Lloyd, Ed Silvoso, and John Gatto, authors and leaders who informed and inspired me to take on this mission. We've never met, but I see through your lens.

Thank you Vince Croft (My Cuzin Vinny) and Patrick Cowherd. You are real brothers and I love you.

Thank you, my incredible friends: Angel Mills, Katie Williams, Will Prude, Monte Hay, Eric White, Michael Morrison, Stephen McLaughlin, Robert & Dawn Lemus, Pat Powers, Dr. Eric Thompson, Sanjay Karani, Sharron Babb, Scott & Shana Falany, Melissa Detwiler, Dr. Kim Bynum, Matthew Currin, Tracy Raulerson, Tim & Angie Brack, Nick Houtt, Melanie Thomas, Jon Awad, Rodney & Jackie Blunt, Bishop Vaughn McLaughlin, Octavious Davis, Dudl Media LLC, Charlie Ugaz, James Brown, Erica Wortherly, Red Smith, Sylvia Grace, Sally Fitfit, Jeff Manin, all Clemson University basketball alumni.

To the many others whom I love, I thank you that you helped inspire this book, and all my future books.

How to Order

To secure Grayson Marshall to <u>speak</u> at your next team, employee, or leadership meeting, conference, retreat, or convention, to <u>order bulk copies</u>, or to <u>request media interviews</u>:

Website: www.graysonmarshalljr.com

Phone: 904-201-4422 ext 101

Email: grayson@graysonmarshalljr.com

If you're a fan of this book please tell others...

- ☐ Write about *Your 2nd Half – The Answer After Sports* on your blog and social media channels.
- ☐ Suggest this book to your friends, family, neighbors, and coworkers.
- ☐ Write a positive review on Amazon.com.
- ☐ Purchase additional copies for your business or sports team, or to give away as gifts.
- ☐ Feature Grayson on your radio or television broadcast.

Other titles from Grayson Marshall:

Do Positive – *The Keys to the Life You Always Imagined*

Only the top 3% of individuals achieve success using today's principles and personal development tools. Experience significant, immediate changes through a genuine understanding and awareness of how you think. This is not a program – far from it. Discover why we feel uncomfortable when trying new things and how to build new, broader comfort zones. Understand habits and how to change them. Have an ah-ha moment about goal setting. Free yourself from the cycles that stop you from achieving the life you've always imagined.

Maintaining Greatness – *Managing your Gifts for Limitless Living*

You were born great and somehow have lost sight of it. Would you like to have it back? What about living a life if service which leads to Greatness? Doing this is the act of reclaiming your birthright and rightfully positioned in the place of blessing. This book will outline and highlight the required change and positive checklist for you return. If you understand and apply what lies in the pages of this book you will forever learn and be reminded daily of the importance of Maintaining Greatness and the power, freedom, and peace in being what you were born to be.

Grayson's Programs:

ARE YOU READY TO CHANGE YOUR ORGANIZATION OR TEAM?

SUCCESSFULLY NAVIGATING THE NEW HIGH SCHOOL SPORTS EXPERIENCE

The amateur label that used to describe high sports is no more. High school sports are "BIG" business now and the rules of engagement of completely different. The Exposure is more frequent, the money has gone to the billions and the expectation and element of entitlement have total changed the experience. The lack of knowledge and understanding is affecting young athletes like never before. We have a program both face to face and online that allow insight and a strategy plan to navigate the new playing field. Parents and student athletes alike benefit from this program. Contact us today and let us do for you and you athletes what we are doing for so many.

THE LOCKER ROOM EXPERIENCE - For Coaches Only

The responsibility that coaches have today is vastly different today. The position of mentor, life director and father figure are being shared and often taken by people more involved in the sports business rather than the coaching business. The Locker Room Experience is a program to reinvent the coach to have even more impact today and equip them to be more versed on how to communicate with the entitled athlete of today that is being influenced by a business set exploit and use them. You coach because you care, let us help you do it with even more confidence and faith.

MAINTAINING GREATNESS - THE IMMERSION EXPERIENCE

The key to growing personally understands that greatness has been in you since birth. We often feel like we are out to become great but in essence you already are so the quest is to begin to understand that and once it is embraced and realized the challenge is how to Maintain it. These "Immersion Experience goes deeper into you and your personal belief systems. We identify the road blocks and reiterate your ability to make change and overcome. You don't want to miss these epic events. Look on the calendar and see when the next one is and make sure you are there..

THE LEADING EDGE - Corporate Training

There is such a similarity with corporate America and the element of teams in the sports world. We have been successful in bring the one element of Corporate America that seems to go often unaddressed and that is Leadership. Every good company rises and falls on Leadership. We make sure we align and help to apply team based leadership principles that focus on the personal ownership of each member of the team. We instill a selfless winning attitude into the workplace and empower people to personally grow as the company does. Let us assist you in creating a culture that is the place everyone wants us to work.

www.ingramcontent.com/pod-product-compliance
Lightning Source LLC
Chambersburg PA
CBHW032049150426
43194CB00006B/467